TRUE BREWS

True Brews

How to Craft
FERMENTED CIDER, BEER,
WINE, SAKE, SODA, MEAD,
KEFIR, AND KOMBUCHA
at Home

Emma Christensen

PHOTOGRAPHY BY PAIGE GREEN

TEN SPEED PRESS
Berkeley

Copyright © 2013 by Emma Christensen
Photographs copyright © 2013 by Paige Green

All rights reserved.
Published in the United States by Ten Speed Press, an imprint of the
Crown Publishing Group, a division of Random House, Inc., New York.
www.crownpublishing.com
www.tenspeed.com

Ten Speed Press and the Ten Speed Press colophon are registered
trademarks of Random House, Inc.

Library of Congress Cataloging-in-Publication Data
Christensen, Emma.
    True brews : how to craft fermented cider, beer, wine, sake, soda,
kefir, and kombucha at home / Emma Christensen. — First edition.
        pages cm
    Includes index.
    Summary: "An accessible homebrew guide for alcoholic and
non-alcoholic fermented drinks, including beer, mead, soda, kefir,
kombucha, hard cider, sake, and fruit wines"—Provided by publisher.
1. Brewing—Amateurs' manuals. I. Title.
    TP570.C56 2013
    641.87'3—dc23
                                                    2012034347

Hardcover ISBN: 978-1-60774-338-5
eBook ISBN: 978-1-60774-339-2

Printed in China

Design by Katy Brown
Food styling by Karen Shinto
Prop styling by Esther Feinman

10 9 8 7 6 5 4 3 2 1

First Edition

To Grandma Dola

Contents

INTRODUCTION 1
Brewer's Pantry 3
Brewer's Toolbox 8
Brewer's Handbook 13

CHAPTER 1
SODA POP 21
EXPERT INTERVIEW:
JESSE FRIEDMAN, SODACRAFT 21

Master Soda Recipe 22
Ginger Ale 24
Strawberry Soda 26
Orange Cream Soda 27
Watermelon-Mint Soda 29
Cherry-Lime Soda 30
Grape Soda 32
Grapefruit Soda 34
Root Beer 35

CHAPTER 2
KOMBUCHA 37
EXPERT INTERVIEW:
ERIC CHILDS, KOMBUCHA BROOKLYN 37

Master Kombucha Recipe 38
Peach Iced Tea Kombucha 41
Hibiscus Kombucha 45
Blackberry-Sage Kombucha 46
Honey–Green Tea Kombucha 47
White Tea–Pomegranate Kombucha 48

CHAPTER 3
KEFIR 51
EXPERT INTERVIEW:
NANCY VAN BRASCH HAMREN,
NANCY'S YOGURT 51

Master Milk Kefir Recipe 53
Master Water Kefir Recipe 55
Cherry, Pistachio, and Cardamom Kefir Smoothie 57
Banana-Berry Kefir Smoothie 57
Mango Lassi Kefir Smoothie 59
Ginger-Pear Kefir 60
Coconut Water Kefir 62
Sparkling Raspberry Kefir Wine 63

CHAPTER 4
HARD CIDER 67
EXPERT INTERVIEW:
JEFFREY HOUSE, ACE CIDER 67

Master Hard Cider Recipe 68
Dry Apple Cider 73
Sweet Spiced Mulled Cider 75
Pear Cider 77
Hard Lemonade 79
Jamaican Ginger Beer 82
Pineapple–Brown Sugar Cider 84

CHAPTER 5

BEER 87

EXPERT INTERVIEW:
DANN PAQUETTE, PRETTY
THINGS BEER AND ALE PROJECT 87

Master Beer Recipe 88
Amber Ale 97
IPA 101
Apricot Wheat Ale 104
Saison Farmhouse Ale 107
Gluten-Free Pale Ale 111
Mocha Stout 115

CHAPTER 6

MEAD 119

EXPERT INTERVIEW:
ORON BENARY, BROTHERS
DRAKE MEADERY 119

Master Mead Recipe 120
Dry Mead 123
Chai-Spiced Mead 125
Renaissance Fair Sweet Mead 128
Vanilla-Peach Mead 130
Cranberry Mead 132
Blueberry-Lavender Mead 134

CHAPTER 7

SAKE 137

EXPERT INTERVIEW:
GREG LORENZ, SAKÉONE 137

Master Sake Recipe #1 (Easy) 138
Master Sake Recipe #2 (Advanced) 143
Cloudy Cherry Sake 149
Jasmine Green Tea Sake 151
Meyer Lemon–Thyme Sake 152
Gin-Infused Sake 153

CHAPTER 8

FRUIT WINE 155

EXPERT INTERVIEW:
GLENN FOSTER, TALON WINE BRANDS 155

Master Wine Recipe 156
Plum Wine 159
Strawberry Wine 162
Blackberry Wine 164
Raspberry-Rhubarb Wine 166
Blueberry-Pomegranate Wine 169
Summer Melon Wine 171
Sparkling Sour Cherry Wine 173

Resources 176
Measurement Conversions 177
Acknowledgments 178
About the Author 179
Index 180

Introduction

Let's set a few things straight: anyone can homebrew in any size apartment with a stockpot, a bucket, and a jug. I promise you this is true. You don't need a lot of space. You don't need fancy equipment. You won't stink up the apartment or be forced to hide homebrew in the bathtub. And as long as you use common sense, you don't need to worry about exploding bottles. You want to homebrew? Let's do it.

Sodas run the gamut from the simplest of ginger ales to the fanciest fancy-pants fresh fruit- and herb-infused sparklers. There are kombucha scobys and kefir grains that have traveled the world and back over the course of generations. Homebrewers and winemakers will argue into the wee hours about the merits of this brewing technique with that temperature variance and using this particular piece of hand-welded equipment.

But every single one of these brews, from that basic soda to the finest Pinot Noir, shares the same fundamental process. If you take a sugary liquid, add some yeast or friendly bacteria, and let it sit for a while without bothering it, this beverage will transform into something fizzy, flavorful, and quite often, alcoholic. That, my friends, is fermentation.

Sugary liquid + yeast (and the occasional friendly bacteria) + time = delicious fermented beverage

It really is that simple. Right this very minute, you could buy a gallon of grape juice from the store, add a teaspoon of yeast, and in a few weeks, you'd have wine. Not very good wine, but wine nonetheless. If you want better wine, there are some details that need to be discussed. Lucky for you, those details are right here in this book.

I started brewing beer in 2009 with my husband. We were newly married and newly settled in a city far away from friends and family. We thought that brewing would be a dandy project to tackle as we settled into our new life together.

Our first batch was so terrible that we poured it straight down the drain. Our second batch was slightly better. Our third was downright drinkable. By our fourth, we had upgraded our equipment, collected a small library of brewing books, and reserved the domain name for our imaginary future brewpub: New Low Brewing Company. (Its tagline: "When life reaches a new low, grab the beer that's right there with you!")

As was probably inevitable, I started looking around for more things that we could transform into alcohol using this magical process of fermentation. I grilled a friend about making mead and started obsessing over the idea of brewing sake. Yeast-carbonated sodas in recycled plastic bottles started collecting in our fridge. After a second move, this one to California,

I discovered kombucha and kefir. I loved these beverages immediately for their snappy flavors and centuries-old fermentation process—plus their payload of probiotics and antioxidants didn't hurt.

At a certain point, it became obvious: I was addicted to brewing. Which, in the larger scheme of things, is not really so terrible.

All of the recipes in this book are tailored to batches of 1 gallon or less. That goes for the equipment as well as the ingredients. I have only ever lived in small city apartments, and so I sympathize with the limits on kitchen and storage space.

Small batches are also good for learning the brewing process. Temperatures are easier to control, pots are easier to lift, and mistakes are easier to catch. And if a mistake does happen somewhere in the process, it's less heartbreaking to part with 1 gallon of funky brew than 5 or more of them.

The Brewer's Pantry, Brewer's Toolbox, and Brewer's Handbook sections are meant to introduce you to the basic ingredients, equipment, and procedures you'll encounter in the recipes that follow. Flip through them before you get started so you know what you're shopping for. Later on, use these sections for refining your skills and tweaking your process.

The ensuing chapters start with the easiest and quickest brewing recipes and move gradually to the more lengthy: soda pop, kombucha, kefir, hard cider, beer, mead, sake, and fruit wine. Interviews with some of the top brewers and artisan makers in the country kick off each chapter, giving you expert advice and inspiration as you dive into your own brewing projects.

The master recipes are there to guide you through the individual quirks and procedures for each brew in extensive detail. They are also your template for making your own recipes. If you discover an abandoned apricot tree or find yourself unable to resist a flat of olallieberries at the farmers' market, you can adapt your bounty to these master recipes and feel confident in the results.

And of course, there are the recipes themselves. I'm probably not supposed to pick favorites, but promise me you'll try the Watermelon-Mint Soda (page 29) this summer along with the Apricot Wheat Ale (page 104). The Strawberry Wine (page 162) and Summer Melon Wine (page 171) are also excellent for sipping in the middle of winter when you need a reminder of what sun feels like. One more? Make the Sweet Spiced Mulled Cider (page 75). You won't regret it.

I hope these recipes and this book as a whole inspire your brewing and give you the tools to start experimenting on your own. Your tastes and my tastes may not be exactly the same all the time, and you may very well encounter brewing snags that I couldn't anticipate when working on these recipes in my own kitchen. But stick with it. Talk to other homebrewing friends. Experiment. And most of all, have yourself a grand old time. There's nothing more rewarding than pouring yourself a glass of homebrew and drinking every single drop.

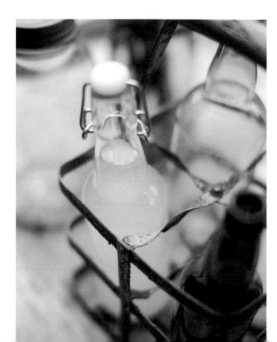

BREWER'S PANTRY

It never ceases to amaze me how such complex and deeply flavored beverages can be made from just a few basic ingredients. Nothing fancy is needed: just some fruit or maybe some malts for beer, sugar, water, and yeast. Plus a few other ingredients to round things out.

Basic Brewing Ingredients

Here we have the heavy hitters, the basic brewing ingredients you'll use again and again. Keep them stocked and you'll never lack for something to brew.

FRUIT

Fruit forms the base of the vast majority of recipes in this book and the vast majority of fermented beverages in general. It is worth seeking out the very best you can find and afford.

CANNED FRUIT. Canned fruit should be a last resort. Most are packed with sugar and preservatives, and definitely are no longer at their fruity best. Will they ferment? Yes. Will they taste good? Probably not.

DRIED FRUIT. Dried fruits are best used for smaller brews, like flavoring kefir or adding a bit of fruitiness to a batch of beer.

FRESH FRUIT. When at all possible, use fresh fruit that is ripe and in season. This fruit is guaranteed to be at its very peak in flavor and quality. Taste before buying and only buy fruit that you would eat on its own. Wine made with mediocre strawberries will end up being mediocre strawberry wine.

FROZEN FRUIT. Frozen fruit from the grocery store is second best to fresh. (And fruit you freeze yourself is just as good as fresh!) Obviously, you can't taste frozen fruit before buying it, but use your best judgment. I have found that frozen organic fruits are generally higher in quality than more commercial varieties.

FRUIT JUICE. Good fruit juice is halfway to being cider or wine already! Buy only 100 percent juice products, with no added sugar and preferably no preservatives. Pasteurized juices are fine, but will make your finished brew look hazy.

MALTS

Malted grains, or malts, are used almost exclusively for beer brewing. Hidden inside the little grains are the sugars that will eventually feed the yeast. They're called malted grains for the process by which they're made: grains are partially sprouted, or "malted," to develop their sugars and then dried before being sold. Malts are usually barley, but can also be wheat, rice, oats, corn, or even rye. They can also be lightly toasted or deeply roasted; combining different kinds of malts will change the flavor profile of your beer. Remember to have your grains milled at the brewing supply store when you buy them; this cracks the grains open and exposes their sugary insides to the brewing process.

MILK

Kefir cultures love the fattiness of whole milk but will settle for 2 percent or even non-fat milk. Pasteurized milk is okay, but avoid ultra-high-temperature pasteurized (UHT) milk, which doesn't have enough nutrients for the kefir to survive on. Cow, goat, or sheep milk can be used to make kefir, as can raw milk. (If using raw milk, use only the highest-quality milk coming from a source you trust.) Almond, soy, and other nonanimal milks can also be used, but the kefir grains will wear out after a while; they can either be replaced with new grains or soaked in animal milk to revitalize them (see chapter 3 for more details on making and using kefir).

RICE

The rice used for commercial sake-making is polished to a very high degree, much more than the average table rice that we buy for dinner. You can buy specially milled sake rice online (see Resources, page 176), but short-grain rice or sushi-grade medium-grain rice makes a good substitute, is easier to find, and makes an only slightly less-refined sake. Avoid long-grain rice because its starches are not as easily fermented into sake.

SUGAR

Sugar is yeast food. Yeast need it in order to ferment our brews, produce carbon dioxide to carbonate our brews, and make the alcohol that gives many brews their punch. Some beverages like ciders have enough natural sugars on their own, but most brews need a little help.

Malts

BROWN SUGAR, TURBINADO, AND PILONCILLO. Using these sugars for all or some of the sugar in a recipe will give your brew a caramel-like sweetness even after fermentation.

CORN SUGAR. I don't typically use corn sugar for brewing per se, but it's my favorite kind of sugar to add during bottling to make carbonated beverages. It dissolves easily, is virtually tasteless, and won't affect the flavor of your beverage.

HONEY. Locally produced honeys from equally local bees are going to have a lot more character and complexity than mass-produced honey from the store. I recommend the former over the latter whenever possible. Honey can be substituted for white granulated sugar, though it will give brews a mild honey flavor. Some people like this, others don't—it's up to you. Use about 50 percent more honey than you would sugar (1 cup sugar to 1 1/2 cups honey). Also note that honey lacks some of the essential nutrients that help the yeast thrive, so it's important to add yeast nutrient whenever brewing with honey. *Do not* use honey when brewing lacto-fermented beverages like kefir and kombucha. The antiseptic nature of honey will weaken these cultures over time.

WHITE GRANULATED SUGAR. This is the sugar I use for most brewing projects. It ferments fully and cleanly, meaning the yeast will eat all of the sugar (at least until the alcohol level becomes too high), and it won't leave behind much residual flavor. Everyday grocery-store cane sugar is fine for brewing purposes, though organic is preferred.

WATER

You don't need to get too fancy with your water. As long as the water from your tap tastes good, it will do quite nicely. If desired, you can filter your water or buy it already filtered from the store. For some recipes, you'll need to dechlorinate your water before brewing (see page 14).

YEAST

Any yeast will ferment any beverage, but some yeast strains have been specially developed to work best with particular beverages. For instance, you can use Hefeweizen yeast with wheat beers and Pasteur red wine yeast with red wines. When you're first starting out, stick to what the recipe calls for. Once you're feeling confident, you can start playing around with other yeasts in your brews to see how they affect fermentation and flavor. It's even possible to use wild yeasts to ferment your brew, though the results are harder to predict and control. One tube or pouch of liquid yeast or one packet of dry yeast is enough to ferment up to 5 gallons of homebrew. For this book's 1-gallon batches, you can use half of a tube or half of a pouch of liquid yeast and save the rest in a sanitized sealed jar in the refrigerator for another batch. With dry yeast, it's easiest just to use the whole packet.

Other Brewing Ingredients

These are the supporting actor ingredients, many of which are specific to the world of brewing. You won't find them at your grocery store, but your local homebrew supply store will keep them stocked. If in doubt, turn to the Internet for your supplying needs (see Resources, page 176).

ACID BLEND. This powder gives ciders, meads, sake, and wines their crisp edge. Go by the sweetness of your fruit and add more or less to compensate. You can always add more later if you find that your wine tastes flat.

CAMPDEN TABLETS. This sulfite is used for sterilizing fruit and other ingredients that don't get cooked during the fermentation process, especially with mead and wine. One crushed tablet will do the trick for a 1-gallon batch of homebrew. Since it kills all the bacteria and wild yeast in the fruit, add it to your homebrew 24 hours before pitching (adding) the yeast. A second tablet added before bottling helps to stabilize the wine and prevent further fermentation (and potentially exploding bottles) after bottling. Do not use a second Campden for beverages you plan to carbonate.

DRIED MALT EXTRACT. Use this when making yeast starters for beer. Dried malt extract is basically über-concentrated beer juice that has been dried into a powder.

HOPS. These fragrant flowers play a big role making beer but can also be used for flavoring mead, sake, and wine. Available as compressed pellets or (more rarely) as whole fresh hop flowers, they help to balance the sweetness of the malts and preserve the beer so it stays fresh longer. Hops contain two things: resins that add bitterness and oils that add flavors and aromas. Hops have to be boiled for a lengthy period

of time to extract the bittering resins, but this same boiling will destroy the more delicate flavoring and aroma oils. This is why hops are usually added at three times: hops at the start of the boil for bittering, hops in the last 20 minutes or so for flavoring, and hops at the very end for aroma. The same or different hops can be used at all three stages depending on which flavors and aromas you desire in the finished brew.

IRISH MOSS. When you want a very clear beer, add a pinch of dried Irish moss during the last 20 minutes of the hop boil. This seaweed (also called carragheen or carrageen) helps to settle out the proteins that cause hazy beers.

KEFIR GRAINS. Similar to a kombucha scoby, kefir grains are home to the bacteria and yeasts that ferment kefir. There are two different kinds of kefir grains: milk kefir grains that ferment the lactose in milk and that look like miniature cauliflowers, and water kefir grains that ferment white granulated sugar and look more like rubbery crystals. Both kinds of kefir grains are gluten-free and are reusable from batch to batch. You can find dehydrated kefir grains online (see Resources, page 176).

KOJI RICE. Necessary for sake brewing, this rice has been inoculated with a special mold that breaks down rice starches into sugar to feed the yeast. You can make it yourself (see page 146) or buy prepared koji rice (see Resources, page 176).

This page, top to bottom: Hops; kefir grains; koji rice
Opposite page: Scoby

PECTIC ENZYME. Some fruits that are high in pectin will cause a haze in the wine or cider (which is called, predictably, "pectin haze"). This powder helps to clear the pectin and give you a crystal-clear brew. Since it's hard to tell how much pectin any given fruit will have, it's good practice to add $1/2$ teaspoon to every 1-gallon batch of wine at the beginning of fermentation regardless of the fruit being used.

SCOBY. Technically, scoby stands for "symbiotic culture of bacteria and yeast." It's also sometimes called a mother or a kombucha mushroom. The scoby looks like a thick, rubbery, cream-colored disk, and it houses all the bacteria and yeast that go into brewing kombucha. The same scoby can be reused in each batch of kombucha. You can buy them online (see Resources, page 176) or grow your own (see How to Make Your Own Scoby, page 42).

TANNIN. Tannin is responsible for the sensation of dryness and astringency in your mouth when drinking wine, similar to the feeling of drinking a strong cup of black tea. As strange as this may sound, a few pinches of this powder help give ciders, meads, and wines an overall balanced quality. You'll miss it if it's not there! Some fruits have their own natural tannin (like blackberries) and others need a little more help. Start with a little; you can add more later in the process if you decide you want a drier-tasting wine.

YEAST NUTRIENT. Yeast requires a few essential nutrients to thrive, and unfortunately, these are lacking in the fruit and sugar going into ciders, meads, sake, and wine. The added nutrient, which comes as a powder, gives the yeast the extra vitamins and minerals it needs to stay happy.

BREWER'S TOOLBOX

I am a big proponent of using the pots, pans, and tools you already have. If your mom gave you a stockpot when you moved into your first apartment and it still holds water, by all means use it. This said, it's worth buying whatever equipment you don't have. Don't try to get by with a tea strainer in place of a bigger strainer or guess the number of cups with a coffee mug. You'll just drive yourself crazy.

The brewing-specific equipment like bottle cappers and jugs are available at homebrewing supply stores and online. Take a look at the Resources section at the end of the book (page 176) if you're having trouble finding something in particular.

Brewing Equipment

Gather these materials when you're ready to get your brew on.

ELECTRONIC SCALE. Precision is key for many recipes, and weighing ingredients is much more accurate than scooping them. Buy a scale that can toggle between grams and ounces, and that can register weight as small as 5 grams or $1/4$ ounce.

» USE FOR: cider, beer, mead, sake, wine

FLOUR SACK TOWELS OR CHEESECLOTH. Flour sack towels are large pieces of tightly woven cloth that can be washed and reused. They're useful for things like steaming rice for sake and for straining out fruit and other sediment from your brews. Cheesecloth can also be used but should be doubled a few times to make a finer weave.

» USE FOR: beer, mead, sake, wine

LARGE FINE-MESH STRAINER. Buy one that's big enough to rest over your stockpot and fermentation bucket. A metal strainer with a long handle and a deep well that's about 10 inches in diameter is ideal.

» USE FOR: beer, mead, sake, wine

LONG-HANDLED SPOON. You'll use this constantly during all stages of the brewing process and for every brew. Make sure it reaches to the very bottom of the pot (without submerging your hand in boiling liquid, of course). Plastic, silicone, or metal spoons are best since they are easily cleaned and sanitized.

» USE FOR: soda, kombucha, kefir, cider, beer, mead, sake, wine

MEASURING CUPS AND SPOONS. Since you'll be measuring large quantities of water, it's very useful to have a quart (4-cup) or larger liquid measuring cup in addition to standard 1-cup and $1/2$-cup measures. Tablespoon and teaspoon measures are necessary for accurately measuring out small quantities of spices, additives, and other brewing ingredients.

» USE FOR: soda, kombucha, kefir, cider, beer, mead, sake, wine

SANITIZING SOLUTION. For ciders, beers, meads, sake, and wines, you need to sanitize all equipment coming into contact with your brew at every stage of the process (for beer, sanitation is important once the hop boil is complete). All homebrewing stores carry instant sanitizers that just need to be diluted in water. Some good ones are One-Step and StarSan. You can also use a solution of 1 tablespoon of bleach to 1 gallon of cold water and soak equipment for 20 minutes. Be sure to rinse the beach solution off the equipment before using it. (See How to Sanitize Your Equipment, page 14.)

» USE FOR: cider, beer, mead, sake, wine

SMALL FINE-MESH STRAINER. A small $3^1/_2$-inch-diameter strainer is very helpful for filtering out sediment from soda or straining kefir grains. Make sure your strainer is plastic or stainless steel since aluminum and other reactive metals can give brews a metallic flavor and will weaken kefir and kombucha cultures over time.

» USE FOR: soda, kombucha, kefir, sake

STOCKPOT. A 2-gallon pot is big enough for all of the recipes, though some of the beers will be a tight fit. If you already have a 2-gallon pot, start with that. If you're buying one new, spring for a 12-quart (3-gallon) pot.

» USE FOR: kombucha, hard cider, beer, mead, sake, wine

THERMOMETER. Some brews need to be heated or cooled to certain temperatures at certain times. I like to use a digital instant-read thermometer because it's quick and accurate, but a mercury-based candy thermometer is also fine. An oven thermometer is also handy for the mash step in brewing beer.

» USE FOR: cider, beer, mead, sake, wine

Fermentation Equipment

You'll need some special equipment for the actual fermentation stage of brewing. These things will keep your homebrew safe from bacteria, oxygen, and dust while it's fermenting away.

AIR LOCK. Inserted into the lid of the fermentation bucket (and later, the jug), an air lock allows carbon dioxide to escape while preventing dust, bacteria, and other undesirables from coming in contact with the brew.

» USE FOR: cider, beer, mead, sake, wine

Top to bottom: Stockpot, long-handled spoon, thermometer; large fine-mesh strainer, clear 2-gallon plastic food storage container; airlock

CANNING JARS. Canning jars are cheap, easy to clean and sanitize, and come in lots of different sizes. They are perfect for lots of little brewing tasks.

» USE 1-GALLON CANNING JARS FOR: kombucha, sake
» USE 2-QUART CANNING JARS FOR: kombucha, water kefir, sake
» USE 1-PINT CANNING JARS FOR: milk kefir, cider, beer, mead, sake, wine

FINE-MESH 19-INCH BAG. Keeping fruits contained in one of these nylon or muslin mesh bags makes it infinitely easier to strain out the solids after fermentation.

» USE FOR: cider, mead, wine

FOOD-GRADE 2-GALLON PLASTIC BUCKET WITH LID. This is your "primary fermenter." Although we're brewing 1-gallon or smaller batches, a 2-gallon bucket is the way to go. This will hold all the fermenting liquid plus any fruits or other ingredients you choose to add. A larger bucket also gives the fermenting brew more space to bubble and froth during the first few very active days of fermentation without risk of the brew spilling out of the bucket. Make sure the lid has a rubber-lined hole for the air lock. If your local homebrew store doesn't carry this size, you can find them online or at hardware stores, though you may have to drill and grommet the lid yourself.

» USE FOR: cider, beer, mead, sake, wine

LARGE FUNNEL. Use this when transferring brews with a lot of sediment into the secondary fermenter. Lined with a flour sack towel, it helps filter out the solids. An 8-inch funnel is ideal.

» USE FOR: mead, sake, wine

Top to bottom: Food-grade 2-gallon plastic bucket with lid, cheesecloth; racking cane and tip for the racking cane; 1-gallon glass jug, siphon hose, and hose clamp

1-GALLON GLASS JUG. This is your "secondary fermenter." After the main fermentation is done, you'll transfer your brew into this smaller container for longer aging and to minimize contact with oxygen. Some homebrew stores sell 4-liter jugs instead of 1-gallon ones. These will hold just slightly more liquid and are fine to use.

» USE FOR: cider, beer, mead, sake, wine

JUG STOPPER. You'll need a plastic stopper, like a cork, to fit in the neck of your 1-gallon jug. Make sure it has a hole drilled through the middle for the air lock. One-gallon jugs generally take a #6 stopper (the number refers to the size).

» USE FOR: cider, beer, mead, sake, wine

RACKING CANE. This crooked tube made of either plastic or glass looks a little like a miniature version of your grandma's walking cane. Choose one that is 16 to 24 inches in length and use this for creating a siphon to transfer brews from one container to the next, aka "racking."

» USE FOR: cider, beer, mead, sake, wine

TIP FOR THE RACKING CANE. This little cap fits over the end of the racking cane and helps prevent sediment from the bottom of the fermentation bucket and jug from being pulled into the tube.

» USE FOR: cider, beer, mead, sake, wine

SIPHON HOSE. Another part of the siphon, this length of plastic tubing gets attached to the racking cane and later to the bottle filler. Buy at least 3 feet of $^5/_{16}$-inch plastic tubing and make sure that it will fit over the tip of your racking cane.

» USE FOR: cider, beer, mead, sake, wine

HOSE CLAMP. Slip this over the open end of the siphon hose to help control the flow of liquid through the tube.

» USE FOR: cider, beer, mead, sake, wine

Bottling Equipment

Bottling time! You weren't going to drink from the jug, were you? Not only is it extremely satisfying to behold a shelf of your own homebrew, but bottling makes homebrew easier to store, serve, and share with friends.

BOTTLES. Carbonated beverages, such as soda and beer, need to be bottled in containers made to withstand the pressure of carbonation. These can be reused plastic soda bottles, swing-top bottles, or any bottle that can take a crown cap (generally 12-ounce and 22-ounce beer bottles that have a thin lip around the rim). Additionally, longer-aging brews, such as cider and beer, should be kept in dark-colored bottles to protect them from the light, which can affect flavor. With wines and other still (nonbubbly) beverages, we also have the option of corking in wine bottles.

» USE BROWN 12-OUNCE OR 22-OUNCE GLASS BOTTLES FOR: soda (conditionally, see recipe), cider, beer, mead, sake, wine

» USE SWING-TOP BOTTLES FOR: soda (conditionally, see recipe), kombucha, water kefir, cider, beer, and for short-term storage of mead, sake, and wine

» USE REUSED PLASTIC SODA BOTTLES FOR: soda, kombucha, water kefir, and for short-term storage of cider, beer, mead, sake, wine

» USE 750-MILLILITER WINE BOTTLES FOR: noncarbonated mead, sake, non-carbonated wine

BOTTLE CAPS. You can reuse glass beer bottles indefinitely, but need to use fresh caps with each project.

» USE FOR: cider, beer, mead, sake, wine

BOTTLE CAPPER AND/OR WINE CORKER. Butterfly cappers and basic wine corkers are fairly inexpensive and worth buying for the convenience. Homebrewing stores also usually have full-size wine corkers, which are easier to use than the smaller ones, available for rent.

» USE FOR: cider, beer, mead, sake, wine

BOTTLE FILLER. This is a straight plastic tube with a pressure lock on one end. When pressed against the bottom of a bottle, it will allow liquid to pass through. When lifted, the flow of liquid stops. This little device makes bottling far easier and less messy.

» USE FOR: cider, beer, mead, sake, wine

WINE CORKS. As with bottle caps, fresh corks need to be used every time you bottle, although wine bottles can be reused.

» USE FOR: noncarbonated mead, sake, noncarbonated wine

Other Handy Things

You can certainly brew without these things, but having them makes life easier.

BOTTLE BRUSH. One of these makes cleaning the gunk from the insides of the fermentation jug and bottles a breeze.

CLEAR 2-GALLON PLASTIC FOOD STORAGE CONTAINER. Find one with measurement markings down the side and think of it like a really big measuring cup. Eyeballing a gallon of beer wort is fine, but the more neurotic types among us (and I'll raise my own hand here) like the accuracy this provides.

HYDROMETER. Though not strictly a necessary piece of equipment for brewing, this little tool will help you measure the amount of alcohol in your brew (see page 16).

Top to bottom: Hydrometer; bottle filler; bottle capper

BREWER'S HANDBOOK

//

The specifics will vary, but many of the basic techniques and procedures are the same no matter what you're brewing. All brews start out as a sugary liquid and finish with being portioned out into bottles. Cleanliness is always important. Starting a siphon will inevitably involve a bit of fumbling and cursing. The rest is in the details.

5 Steps to Homebrewed Beverages

1 • MAKE A SUGARY LIQUID. This might mean mixing fruit juice with sugar for a soda pop or dissolving honey into water for mead, but all you're doing is creating a sugar-rich environment for yeast to live in.

2 • ADD THE YEAST OR YEAST STARTER TO THE SUGARY LIQUID AND STIR VIGOROUSLY. The first several hours of yeast life are not actually spent making alcohol, but rather spent multiplying. For those of us who remember high school chemistry, this is an aerobic activity for which the yeast needs oxygen. That's why stirring, shaking, whisking, or otherwise agitating the sugary liquid is necessary to incorporate oxygen into the liquid.

3 • TRANSFER TO THE PRIMARY FERMENTER. For short-term brews like soda, kefir, and kombucha, the transfer is into either a plastic bottle or a large canning jar. For long-term projects like cider, beer, sake, mead, and wine, the primary fermenter is a 2-gallon bucket. Cover the fermentation vessel and let the liquid get its ferment on.

4 • TRANSFER YOUR NEWLY FERMENTED BEVERAGE TO A SECONDARY FERMENTER. Some of the short-term brews mentioned above won't have a secondary fermentation because they are ready to drink. For everything else, we want to transfer the brew into a smaller 1-gallon jug using a siphon. This is called "racking" in brewing parlance, and it gets the brew off the used fruit, spices, and lees (the sludge of spent yeast, proteins, and other unneeded bits from the bottom of the bucket) and into a cozy container with less exposure to oxygen, which can eventually oxidize the brew and dull its flavors.

The brews hang out here for anywhere from 2 weeks to several months as fermentation finishes and aging begins. Yeast thrives at room temperature, but stops once all of the sugars have been consumed or the alcohol level in the beverage becomes too high for the yeast to survive. Other enzymatic activity continues developing the flavor and character of the brew as it ages.

5 • BOTTLE YOUR BREW. With the exception of milk kefir, all of the brews in this book benefit from being bottled and aged for various lengths of time. Sodas, kombuchas, and water kefirs are ready within a day or two, as soon as they are carbonated. Ciders and beers peak between 4 weeks and 6 months after bottling. Meads, sake, and wine can be stored, aged, and enjoyed for months or years. To make fizzy ciders, beers, meads, and wines, a little sugar is added just before bottling. This gives the yeast just enough of a snack to create some carbon dioxide and carbonate the bottled brew.

This goes without saying, but step 6 is to kick back, pop the cap off a bottle of homebrew, and sip it down. Sharing is optional.

How to Measure and Weigh Ingredients

You'll notice that many of the solid ingredients in this book are given in both volume (cups) and weights (ounces). For consistency's sake, the volume is listed first with the weight second, but there are times when you might prefer to measure one way over the other.

For quick batches of soda, kombucha, and kefir, I most often use cups and measuring spoons to measure the relatively small amounts of sugar, water, and other ingredients. Accuracy is less vital in these recipes, and I like the easy convenience of scooping-and-stirring when throwing together something spontaneous (in the case of soda) or that I make so regularly that pulling out the scale each time seems overly complicated (in the case of kombucha and kefir). To measure solid ingredients in cups, teaspoons, or tablespoons, just scoop up the ingredient, shake the cup or spoon slightly, and level out the top with the back of a butter knife. To measure liquid ingredients in cups, use a liquid measuring cup and fill it to the appropriate line. Set the cup on a level surface and look at the line at eye level. Add more liquid or pour some off until the surface of the liquid is even with the line.

With cider, beer, mead, sake, and wine, accurate measuring of all the ingredients is more crucial for ensuring things like proper fermentation and hitting target gravities, so I highly recommend using an electronic scale (see Brewer's Toolbox, page 8). I also find it more convenient to weigh in bulk the larger amounts of ingredients in these recipes rather than keeping track (and then often losing track!) of how many cups I've added. To weigh ingredients on a scale, set a clean bowl on the scale, tare the scale to zero, and pour or scoop your ingredient into the bowl. Once measured, transfer your ingredient into another bowl before weighing other ingredients.

Eagle-eyed brewers may occasionally notice inconsistencies between weight and volume when measuring ingredients for recipes. This can be due to many variables, including the exact brand of ingredient you use, how long the package has been open, and even how humid the air might be on a particular day. These inconsistencies are slight enough that they shouldn't adversely affect any of the recipes. Just measure as accurately as you are able and proceed with worry-free brewing.

How to Sanitize Your Equipment

All of the equipment used to brew cider, beer, mead, sake, and wine needs to be sanitized before being used. (For quicker brewing projects like soda, kefir, and kombucha, it's fine to simply wash the equipment thoroughly with soap and water.)

Fill your 2-gallon bucket partway with water and add sanitizing solution according to its instructions. Put all of your equipment in this bucket to soak: spoons, siphon hose, racking cane, and anything else that will come into contact with the brew. Most sanitizing solutions work on contact and do not need to be rinsed or dried before using. When the bucket is needed for holding the brew, pour the solution into a separate stockpot for later. (Don't forget to sanitize the lid by wedging it in the bucket and rotating to sanitize the entire surface.)

How to Dechlorinate Water

The chlorine present in most tap water can make life difficult for the yeast, resulting in a poor fermentation. If water is going to be added directly to a fermenting homebrew without being boiled first, it needs to be dechlorinated. (The only exception is when brewing sodas, which are generally made in such small batches and are so quick to ferment that they are not affected.)

Chlorine can be removed from water in one of three ways. You can bring the water to a boil and then let it cool before using. You can also let the water sit for about 12 hours before using. In either of these cases, the chlorine will evaporate. The third option is to filter your water, which is fine in small quantities but labor-intensive for the larger batches unless you have the kind of filter that fits over your faucet.

How to Make a Yeast Starter

Making a "starter" lets the yeast acclimate to its new environment, gives it a jump-start on reproduction, and also ensures that the yeast itself is viable. It's not necessary for quick projects like making soda, but it gives you some extra fermentation insurance when making ciders, beers, meads, and wines. Use the same kind of sugar to make the yeast starter as is used in your recipe: honey for meads, dried malt extract for beers, and so on.

To make the starter, sanitize a canning jar or other small container and spoon. Combine the hot water and the sugar (as specified in the recipe) in the jar and stir to dissolve the sugar. When the sugar solution is cool, add the yeast and stir again. (Yeast starters made with honey need a pinch of yeast nutrient to help the yeast begin fermenting.) Cover the jar with plastic wrap secured with a rubber band, and let it sit at room temperature out of direct sunlight for 1 to 12 hours, according to the recipe (generally 1 to 3 hours for dry yeasts or 6 to 12 hours for liquid yeasts). After a few hours, you should see tiny pinprick bubbles popping on the surface and some foam collecting. Dry yeast starters tend to be more visibly active than liquid yeast starters; as long as you see some sign of activity, your yeast is good to go. If you see no activity after 3 hours, repeat this process with new yeast.

What to Do If Fermentation Won't Start or Stops Early

Sometimes brews get fussy. Maybe there's too much sugar and the yeast is overwhelmed, or maybe there aren't enough nutrients for the yeast to get started. Maybe the yeast you were using was old, and, even with an active starter, it wasn't enough to get fermentation going. Maybe the yeast was a little too cold.

Keep a close eye on the air lock. If you don't see a single bubble within 48 hours after pitching the yeast, it's time to take some action. First, check the temperature. If it's chilly in your home, move the fermentation bucket somewhere warmer, ideally around 75°F. Second, add $1/2$ teaspoon of yeast nutrient to the brew and stir vigorously with a sanitized slotted spoon or whisk to incorporate oxygen. Wait 12 hours.

If that still doesn't work, make a second yeast starter. When the starter is active, add a little of the homebrew to the jar. Watch for bubbles to begin popping on the surface of the liquid (a sign that things are fermenting), then add a little more homebrew. Continue waiting, watching for bubbles, and gradually adding more homebrew to the yeast starter until the whole jar is filled, and then stir the starter into the bucket with the remaining homebrew. Stir vigorously to incorporate oxygen into the liquid. You should see signs of fermentation as evidenced by bubbles in the air lock within 12 hours.

If fermentation doesn't start after a second round of yeast starter, something else is going on with the brew. Unfortunately, it's probably best to toss the batch and start again fresh. This happens extremely rarely with small-batch homebrewing.

If fermentation suddenly stops after an active period, first check the gravity of your brew with a hydrometer. It's possible that it's simply done, in which case the gravity reading will be within its Target Final Gravity Range. If you think that there is still some fermenting left to do, follow the same procedure for starting an inactive fermentation as described above. If fermentation doesn't begin again, the brew has likely fermented as much as it's going to, and you can proceed with the rest of the recipe.

How to Use a Hydrometer to Measure Alcohol

A hydrometer measures the density, or "gravity," of liquids relative to that of water and can be used to calculate the amount of alcohol in your homebrew. Since sugary water is denser than plain water, you can take one reading at the beginning of fermentation and another at the end to see how much sugar has been consumed, and therefore how much alcohol has been created.

To use one, fill the hydrometer tube three-quarters full of homebrew, set it on a flat surface, and float the hydrometer inside. Observe where the surface of the liquid hits the hydrometer and record the number.

Before fermentation, the "original gravity" (OG) reading can range from 1.030 to 1.150 for very sugary (and soon-to-be very boozy) homebrews. After brewing, the "final gravity" (FG) reading can range from 1.015 to 1.000. Subtract the final gravity from the original gravity, multiply by 131.25, and you'll have your measure of alcohol by volume (ABV).

Many factors can affect the amount of sugar in your recipes and resultant gravity readings, from the sugar content of the fruit used in a wine recipe to the mash temperature of your beer. Since these factors are variable, I give a target range for you to aim for in the recipes in this book. Don't worry if

you don't hit the target ranges exactly; your "aim" will improve the more you get used to these brewing techniques. Even if you don't hit the targets, you can still use the original and final gravity readings to determine the exact alcohol content of your brew.

One final note: hydrometers are calibrated to work in liquids at 59°F. If your brew is warmer or colder, adjust the gravity reading based on the conversion chart that comes with the hydrometer.

How to Create a Siphon

Siphons make the job of transferring homebrew from container to container much easier, less messy, and with less risk of contaminating the brew. You'll need the racking cane, its tip, a siphon hose, and a hose clamp.

Before you begin siphoning, sanitize everything that will come into contact with the homebrew, including running sanitizer through the hose itself. Place the bucket or jug with your homebrew on the counter and position the empty jug, bucket, or bottles on a chair at least 1½ feet below. If necessary, set the container of homebrew on top of a few books to get the proper elevation.

Attach the hose to the smaller "hook" of the racking cane. Slip the hose clamp over the unattached end of the hose. Run tap water through this end of the hose until it streams fluidly out the other end of the racking cane. Quickly clamp the hose shut, trapping the water inside.

As long as that clamp is closed, the water will stay inside. If you're bottling, attach the bottle filler to the free end of the hose.

Attach the tip to the racking cane and place this inside the container with your homebrew. Lower the open end of the hose into the empty container and release the clamp. This will start a siphon, pulling the homebrew through the hose and into the jug. The small amount of water in the siphon hose won't affect your brew, but if you'd like, siphon into a cup until the hose is clear of water. Tilt the bucket or jug of homebrew toward the end of siphoning to transfer as much as you can and stop when the hose starts becoming cloudy with sediment.

How to Bottle Your Homebrew

One gallon of homebrew gives you about ten 12-ounce beer bottles, or six 22-ounce beer bottles.

Arrange the sanitized bottles on top of a baking sheet or inside a pot to keep them steady during bottling and to catch drips. Prepare your siphon and attach the bottle filler to the open end of the hose (see previous page). Insert the bottle filler into the first bottle and lower it until the tip presses against the bottom of the bottle. Release the hose clamp and fill the bottle. When the liquid reaches the top of the bottle, lift the bottle filler to stop. A mechanism inside the bottle filler will automatically stop the liquid from siphoning without you needing to use the hose clamp. Once the filler is removed from the bottle, you'll also be left with just the right amount of headspace in the neck of the bottle. Repeat with the remaining bottles.

Place all the filled bottles on a flat work surface. Set a cap on top of the opening and lower the bottle capper over the cap. Press down on either side of the capper to crimp the cap around the bottle opening. Repeat with remaining bottles.

How to Cork Wine and Mead in Wine Bottles

Nonsparkling beverages like mead, sake, and wine can be corked in wine bottles. One gallon of homebrew will fill five 750-milliliter wine bottles.

Just before bottling, sanitize the corks. Bring a small amount of water to a boil and add the corks. Simmer for 5 minutes, drain, and set aside on a clean kitchen towel. This process also softens the corks and makes them easier to insert in the wine bottles. Sanitize the bottling equipment and bottles as usual.

Siphon the brew into the wine bottles as described for bottling, leaving about an inch of space at the top of each bottle. With clean hands, insert a cork into the corker, position it over the first bottle, and squeeze the handles to compress the cork and slide it into the neck of the bottle. Repeat with the remaining bottles.

How to Carbonate Any Beverage

Any homebrew with an alcohol content of less than 12 percent can be carbonated. (At higher percentages, the alcohol content usually outpaces the ability of the yeast to continue fermenting and so there won't be enough oomph left to carbonate the brew.) One ounce of corn sugar is enough to carbonate 1 gallon of homebrew.

When you are ready to bottle your homebrew, dissolve the bottling sugar (as specified in the recipe) in $1/2$ cup boiling water. Pour this into a sanitized stockpot. When it has cooled, siphon the homebrew into the pot with the sugar water. This mixes the sugar with the homebrew more thoroughly and evenly than simply pouring it into the jug of homebrew or dividing the sugar water solution among the bottles.

Bottle the homebrew in 12-ounce or 22-ounce bottles with crown caps and wait at least 2 weeks before drinking. The little bit of sugar added before bottling gives the yeast one last kick and produces just enough carbon dioxide to carbonate the brew.

How to Turn Any 1-Gallon Batch into a 5-Gallon Batch

All the recipes in this book, or any home-brew recipe you come across, can be scaled up or down to whatever size batch your homebrewing heart desires. Just keep the proportions of ingredients the same. Also, one tube or one packet of yeast is generally enough to ferment up to 5 gallons of homebrew.

If you increase your batch size, you'll want to pick up a 6-gallon fermentation bucket, a 5-gallon carboy, and for beer, a larger brewing pot. All three are easy to find at homebrew stores. The rest of the equipment is exactly the same.

Exploding Bottles, Funky Smells, and Other Concerns

The only concern you should really have when it comes to homebrewing is "Does this taste good?" Allow me to clear up some of the other worries, fears, and anxieties you may be having so that you can get back to more important matters.

EXPLODING BOTTLES

These recipes all contain very active, very much alive yeasts that would like nothing more than to continue eating all the sugars in your brew. This means that, yes, there is potential for these bottled beverages to gush when you open them (at the very least) or shatter under pressure (at the very worst). Here's how to avoid that:

- FOLLOW THE RECIPE. Refrigerate sodas, kefirs, and kombuchas when the recipe says to in order to halt fermentation and avoid overcarbonation. With the ciders, beers, and other sparkling beverages, a very specific amount of sugar is added before bottling in order to carbonate the brew without over-carbonating. Make sure you measure carefully.

- BOTTLE CARBONATED BEVERAGES IN BOTTLES INTENDED FOR CARBONATED BEVERAGES. There are a lot of really pretty bottles out there, but they aren't all designed to withstand the pressure of carbonated beverages. Bottling in

THE SAFETY AND LEGALITY OF HOMEBREWING

Homebrewed beverages will not make you sick. Even if your vigilance to cleanliness and sanitation suffered a lapse at some point, the acidity and the alcohol content (even if slight) of the liquid will prevent any harmful bacteria or other foodborne illnesses from taking hold. This is not to say that your brew can't become contaminated by outside bugs; it's just that those bugs won't make you physically ill. This said, use your best judgment at all times. If you see mold growing on your kombucha scoby or your beer smells like your sock drawer, best to toss the batch and start over.

Homebrewing is legal in almost all states in the United States, but is restricted to 100 gallons of homebrew per adult or a maximum of 200 gallons per household. Which is really quite enough for any thirsty soul. Unfortunately, homebrewing is still prohibited in some states (for which you can thank Prohibition), so check your state regulations if you are concerned. It is absolutely illegal in all fifty states to sell your homebrew or to distill homebrew. Please don't do either of those things. However, inviting your friends over for a night of merriment and homebrew trading is strongly encouraged.

something not intended for carbonation is just begging for trouble. It's much better to bottle in something safe and then transfer your homebrew to the pretty bottle before serving (see page 31).

- DO NOT LEAVE BOTTLED BREWS IN WARM PLACES. Sodas, kefirs, and kombuchas need to be refrigerated as soon as they are fully carbonated in order to stop the fermentation process. Even if your house, garage, or basement feels cool to you, these beverages will continue to carbonate if the temperature is higher than 35°F. Ciders, beers, meads, sake, and wines can be stored at room temperature (55°F to 80°F) until you want to drink them, but be aware of ambient temperature as the summer comes on. Best places for homebrew storage are basements, interior closets (those that do not share an outside wall with your house or apartment), and low cabinets.

- STORE BOTTLED HOMEBREW INSIDE CUPBOARDS OR BOXES. If the worst happens and a bottle does shatter under pressure, a container will keep the mess to a minimum and keep you safe.

FUNKY SMELLS

Yes, brewing will create some interesting aromas in your house, but you don't need to worry about your landlord knocking on the door. Brewing beer creates a strong smell of malts and hops, but this dissipates quickly once the beer has been transferred to the fermenter. Other brews may smell tantalizingly of cooked fruit as they are being prepared but otherwise have no aroma.

Homebrews will have some yeasty aromas as they ferment, particularly in the first few days of very active fermentation, but the smell is fairly subtle and localized to the area right around the fermentation bucket. If you're concerned, place your brew near an open window or an outside door. Or, yes, you can go old-school and brew in the bathtub.

Brewing in Hot Weather, Brewing in Cold Weather

Brews are very temperature sensitive. If at all possible, keep the environment where your homebrew is fermenting at a steady, comfortable room temperature. A solid 70°F is ideal, but brews are typically fine in a range from 65° to 85°F.

At higher temperatures, like at the peak of summer, fermentation will happen very quickly and be much more active than usual. You may notice that these homebrews lack the same aromatic qualities or have stronger fruity, cider-y, or butterscotch flavors than those brewed in milder temperatures.

The concern at lower temperatures is getting the yeast to ferment at all. Aside from lager yeast and sake yeast, which are designed to work in cooler temperatures, most yeasts get sluggish when the temperature dips much below 60°F. If you're having trouble getting fermentation started or it seems really slow, try moving the fermentation bucket somewhere warmer. On the plus side, brews fermented at cooler temperatures usually have much cleaner and smoother flavors.

CHAPTER 1

Soda Pop

EXPERT INTERVIEW

Jesse Friedman, founder of SodaCraft, San Francisco, California

How did you get hooked on brewing sodas?

As a homebrewer, I had been making special batches of beer for friends' weddings, with ginger ale as a nonalcoholic option. I noticed the ginger ale started running out before the beer! When a new underground market opened in San Francisco (New Taste Marketplace), I started up the soda business, and it caught fire really quickly.

What is your soda-making philosophy?

Our sodas are naturally fermented using yeast for carbonation, and we try as much as possible to be micro-seasonal with the flavors. The sodas are really based on going to the market and seeing which fruits are peaking that day. Everything is juiced fresh by hand and then combined with simple syrup to sweeten.

What is the trickiest aspect of soda-making to master?

Getting consistency between batches. We also limit ourselves to only using produce from local farms, so if our ginger farmer is out of ginger, then we're out of luck with our ginger ale.

What is inspiring you right now?

Single-origin styles. The ones that focus on a single item from a single farm. Originally, I had these ideas of doing wacky, exciting, semisavory flavors, but quickly discovered that even adventurous eaters were weirded out by those sodas. So we went the other way with super simple, straightforward flavors. People really respond to that.

What goes into making a new soda flavor?

It's a mix of instinct and our base recipe. We build off of that base recipe, and then it's all taste. We make a test batch and then tweak it and adjust it.

What is one thing homebrewers could do to improve their sodas?

Get a really good juicer for fresh fruit. That's so helpful. Also, start with really, really good ingredients. The megamart fruit is going to taste like it was grown on the other side of the world. If you can start with fresh fruits that are really popping with flavor, you'll end up with better soda every time.

SODACRAFT SODAS TO TRY: apple cider soda, ginger ale, whatever is in season

Master Soda Recipe

MAKES ABOUT 8 CUPS
(ENOUGH TO FILL A 2-LITER PLASTIC SODA BOTTLE)

Fizzy, fresh sodas can be made from almost anything. No, I take it back: Soda can be made from literally anything. Steep ginger in sugar syrup, and you can make ginger ale. Grab some fresh fruit juice at the farmers' market, and you'll have a soda by morning. Add spices or herbs, mix fruits together, play with savory ingredients, try a different kind of sugar—it's all fair game here.

Base the amount of fruit you use in this recipe on your own personal preferences. Less fruit will give you a lighter-tasting soda, and more fruit will make something closer to nonalcoholic sparkling cider. All sodas need a little lemon juice for punch, but add more if your fruit lacks natural acidity. The amount of sugar you add is entirely up to you and your sweet tooth.

INGREDIENTS

2 to 4 pounds fresh or frozen fruit, or 4 to 8 cups fruit juice, preferably unsweetened

2 to 6 tablespoons freshly squeezed lemon or lime juice (from 1 to 2 lemons or 3 to 4 limes)

1 cup water, plus more to fill the bottles

½ to 1½ cups / 3½ to 10½ ounces white granulated sugar

Flavoring extras: fresh gingerroot, lemon zest, cinnamon stick, star anise, fresh herbs

Pinch of salt

⅛ teaspoon dry champagne yeast

EQUIPMENT

Large bowl

Saucepan

Measuring cups and spoons

Long-handled spoon

Food processor or blender

Large fine-mesh strainer

Flour sack towel or cheesecloth (optional)

Funnel

Small fine-mesh strainer

Clean 2-liter soda bottle with screw cap

YEASTS FOR MAKING SODA

Dry champagne and ale yeasts are my preference for brewing sodas. They ferment easily and don't create any yeasty flavors that would muddy the flavor of the soda itself. But if you're desperate for soda, everyday active dry yeast used for making bread will do in a pinch. However, sodas made with baker's yeast tend to taste more yeasty.

1 • Remove any stems, seeds, peels, or other inedible bits from the fruit and chop into bite-size pieces. Berries and smaller fruits can be kept whole. Combine the fruit with the lemon juice and any flavoring extras in a large bowl.

2 • Bring the water to a boil in a small saucepan on the stove top or in the microwave. Remove from the heat. Add the sugar and salt, stir to dissolve, and pour over the fruit. Let this stand for 10 minutes to macerate the fruit or until frozen fruits are completely thawed. Remove any whole spices once the fruit is macerated. If using fruit juice, simply combine the juice with the sugar water and move to the bottling step.

3 • Working in batches, puree the fruit with its liquid in the food processor or blender. Strain the puree into a bowl, collecting as much juice as possible without forcing any solids through the strainer. You can also strain the juice through a flour sack towel or cheesecloth to yield a soda with less pulp and sediment.

4 • Pour the juice into the clean 2-liter bottle using the funnel. Top off the bottle with water, leaving at least 1 inch of headspace. Give it a taste and add more lemon juice or sugar if desired. The extra sugar will dissolve on its own.

BOTTLING TIP

Sodas can also be bottled in glass or swing-top bottles, just like beer (see page 11), but it's more difficult to tell when the sodas have fully carbonated. Therefore, with every batch you bottle, also fill one small plastic soda bottle to use as an indicator for when the sodas have finished carbonating. Refrigerate all of the bottles as soon as the plastic bottle is carbonated; never leave the glass bottles at room temperature once carbonated.

5 • Add the yeast. Screw on the cap and shake the bottle to dissolve and distribute the yeast. Let the bottle sit at room temperature out of direct sunlight until carbonated, typically 12 to 48 hours. Exact fermentation time will depend on the temperature in the room; soda will carbonate quickly at warm temperatures and take longer at cooler temperatures. Check the bottle periodically; when it feels rock solid with very little give, it's ready.

6 • Refrigerate overnight or for up to 2 weeks. Open very slowly over a sink to release the pressure gradually and avoid bubble-ups. Pour through a small fine-mesh strainer when serving to remove fruit pulp and sediment, if desired.

Ginger Ale

MAKES ABOUT 8 CUPS
(ENOUGH TO FILL A 2-LITER PLASTIC SODA BOTTLE)

Ginger ale was the first soda I ever tried homebrewing, and it was an epiphany. The flavor of the ginger was so bright and clean. The squeeze of lemon complemented it perfectly, and the sugar rounded out the edges. It made my tongue tingle in the best possible way. I can't help but think that this is what ginger ale was meant to taste like.

2-inch piece fresh gingerroot

1 cup water, plus more to fill the bottles

9 tablespoons / 4 ounces white granulated sugar, plus more if needed

⅛ teaspoon salt

5 tablespoons freshly squeezed lemon juice (from 2 to 3 lemons), plus more if needed

⅛ teaspoon dry champagne yeast

HOW TO MAKE SUGAR-FREE SODA

Unless your fruit is very sweet on its own, you will likely need some kind of sweetener to make your soda palatable. You need to use a little real sugar to feed the yeast and carbonate the soda (1 tablespoon white granulated sugar per 8 cups soda), but beyond that, you can sweeten to taste with another sweetener of your choosing.

1 • Peel and finely grate the ginger (I use a Microplane). You should have about 2 tablespoons of grated gingerroot.

2 • Bring the water to a boil in a small saucepan on the stove top or in the microwave. Remove from the heat. Add the sugar and salt and stir to dissolve. Add the ginger and let stand until cool. Stir in the lemon juice.

3 • Pour the ginger water into a clean 2-liter bottle using a funnel. Do not strain out the ginger. Top off the bottle with water, leaving at least 1 inch of headspace. Give it a taste and add more lemon juice or sugar if desired. The extra sugar will dissolve on its own.

4 • Add the yeast. Screw on the cap and shake the bottle to dissolve and distribute the yeast. Let the bottle sit at room temperature out of direct sunlight until carbonated, typically 12 to 48 hours, depending on the temperature of the room. Check the bottle periodically; when it feels rock solid with very little give, it's ready.

5 • Refrigerate overnight or for up to 2 weeks. Open very slowly over a sink to release the pressure gradually and avoid bubble-ups. Pour the soda through a small fine-mesh strainer to catch the ginger as you pour.

Strawberry Soda

MAKES ABOUT 8 CUPS
(ENOUGH TO FILL A 2-LITER PLASTIC SODA BOTTLE)

If you want to taste summer in a bottle, make this soda. Make it with strawberries that are so ripe, they're already halfway to becoming jam. The ones with hard white middles won't do. Make it also for the express purpose of hosting a backyard picnic and for sharing with friends. If you happen to have some tequila handy, try adding a shot to your next glass.

2 pounds fresh or frozen strawberries

¼ cup freshly squeezed lemon juice (from 1 to 2 lemons), plus more if needed

1 cup water, plus more to fill the bottles

9 tablespoons / 4 ounces white granulated sugar, plus more if needed

Pinch of salt

⅛ teaspoon dry champagne yeast

ALCOHOL IN HOMEBREWED SODAS, KEFIRS, AND KOMBUCHAS

As long as yeast is being used to ferment or carbonate beverages, alcohol will be made as a by-product. However, the short fermentation time limits the amount of alcohol produced in sodas, kefirs, and kombuchas, and it usually comes out to less than 1 percent.

1 • Hull and coarsely chop the strawberries. Combine them with the lemon juice in a large bowl.

2 • Bring the water to a boil in a small saucepan on the stove top or in the microwave. Remove from the heat. Add the sugar and salt, stir to dissolve, and pour over the strawberries. Let this stand for 10 minutes to macerate the fruit. If using frozen strawberries, macerate until the strawberries are completely thawed.

3 • Working in batches, puree the strawberries with their liquid in a food processor or blender. Strain the puree into a bowl, collecting as much juice as possible without forcing any solids through the strainer.

4 • Pour the strawberry juice into a clean 2-liter bottle using a funnel. Top off the bottle with water, leaving at least 1 inch of headspace. Give it a taste and add more lemon juice or sugar, if desired. The extra sugar will dissolve on its own.

5 • Add the yeast. Screw on the cap and shake the bottle to dissolve and distribute the yeast. Let the bottle sit at room temperature out of direct sunlight until carbonated, typically 12 to 48 hours, depending on the temperature of the room. Check the bottle periodically; when it feels rock solid with very little give, it's ready.

6 • Refrigerate overnight or for up to 2 weeks. Open very slowly over a sink to release the pressure gradually and avoid bubble-ups.

Orange Cream Soda

MAKES ABOUT 8 CUPS
(ENOUGH TO FILL A 2-LITER PLASTIC SODA BOTTLE)

Guess what makes cream sodas creamy? Go on, guess. Don't cheat by looking down at the ingredients list! Okay, I'll tell you: It's vanilla. The creaminess is less texture and more flavor, tricking your taste buds into thinking otherwise. For a Friday night soda to go with pizza, using vanilla extract is just fine. But if you want to get really fancy, try steeping a split vanilla bean in the sugar water instead.

1 cup water, plus more to fill the bottles

1⅛ cups / 8 ounces white granulated sugar, plus more if needed

Pinch of salt

Zest from 2 oranges

1 teaspoon vanilla extract, or 1 split vanilla bean

2 tablespoons freshly squeezed lemon juice (from 1 lemon), plus more if needed

⅛ teaspoon dry champagne yeast

1 • Bring the water to a boil in a small saucepan on the stove top or in the microwave. Remove from the heat. Add the sugar and salt and stir to dissolve. Add the orange zest (and vanilla bean, if using) and let stand until cool. Stir in the lemon juice and vanilla extract (if using).

2 • Pour the orange water into a clean 2-liter bottle using a funnel. Do not strain out the orange zest. Top off the bottle with water, leaving at least 1 inch of headspace. Give it a taste and add more lemon juice or sugar, if desired. The extra sugar will dissolve on its own.

3 • Add the yeast. Screw on the cap and shake the bottle to dissolve and distribute the yeast. Let the bottle sit at room temperature out of direct sunlight until carbonated, typically 12 to 48 hours, depending on the temperature of the room. Check the bottle periodically; when it feels rock solid with very little give, it's ready.

4 • Refrigerate overnight or for up to 2 weeks. Open very slowly over a sink to release the pressure gradually and avoid bubble-ups. Pour the soda through a small fine-mesh strainer to catch the orange zest as you pour.

Watermelon-Mint Soda

MAKES ABOUT 8 CUPS
(ENOUGH TO FILL A 2-LITER PLASTIC SODA BOTTLE)

Watermelon and mint are total best friends forever. They don't seem like they should go together, what with watermelon's sweet sugary charms and mint's tendency toward sharpness. But somehow they make it work. Besides tasting fantastic together, is there anything prettier than flecks of green mint floating in bubbly pink soda?

4 pounds seeded and cubed watermelon (11 to 12 cups, from a 6-pound watermelon)

½ cup packed fresh mint leaves

½ cup freshly squeezed lime juice (from about 4 limes), plus more if needed

1 cup water, plus more to fill the bottles

9 tablespoons / 4 ounces white granulated sugar, plus more if needed

Pinch of salt

⅛ teaspoon dry champagne yeast

1 • Combine the watermelon, mint leaves, and lime juice in a large bowl.

2 • Bring the water to a boil in a small saucepan on the stove top or in the microwave. Remove from the heat. Add the sugar and salt, stir to dissolve, and pour over the watermelon. Let this stand for 10 minutes to macerate the fruit.

3 • Working in batches, puree the watermelon and mint with their liquid in a food processor or blender. Strain the puree into a bowl, collecting as much juice as possible without forcing any solids through the strainer.

4 • Pour the juice into a clean 2-liter bottle using a funnel. Top off the bottle with water, leaving at least 1 inch of headspace. Give it a taste and add more lime juice or sugar, if desired. The extra sugar will dissolve on its own.

5 • Add the yeast. Screw on the cap and shake the bottle to dissolve and distribute the yeast. Let the bottle sit at room temperature out of direct sunlight until carbonated, typically 12 to 48 hours, depending on the temperature of the room. Check the bottle periodically; when it feels rock solid with very little give, it's ready.

6 • Refrigerate overnight or for up to 2 weeks. Open very slowly over a sink to release the pressure gradually and avoid bubble-ups.

Cherry-Lime Soda

MAKES ABOUT 8 CUPS
(ENOUGH TO FILL A 2-LITER PLASTIC SODA BOTTLE)

I love the tag-team effect of this soda. First, you taste the deep sweetness of those plump summer cherries. Then, just as the cherry is veering toward sticky, the lime juice sweeps in with a fresh citrus burst. Sip after sip, first cherry and then lime. Inspired by the countless cherry-lime rickeys I've enjoyed over the years, I can't get enough of this combo.

2 pounds fresh or frozen sweet cherries, or 6 cups cherry juice

½ cup freshly squeezed lime juice (from about 4 limes), plus more if needed

1 cup water, plus more to fill the bottles

9 tablespoons / 4 ounces white granulated sugar, plus more if needed

Pinch of salt

⅛ teaspoon dry champagne yeast

1 • Pit the cherries, if necessary, and coarsely chop. Combine the fruit with the lime juice in a large bowl.

2 • Bring the water to a boil in a small saucepan on the stove top or in the microwave. Remove from the heat. Add the sugar and salt, stir to dissolve, and pour over the fruit. Let this stand for 10 minutes to macerate the cherries, or until frozen cherries are completely thawed. If using fruit juice, simply combine the juice with the sugar water and skip to the bottling step.

HOW TO AVOID GUSHING, EXPLODING, OVERCARBONATED SODAS

Sodas can overcarbonate very easily. This can cause geysers when you first open them or bursting bottles if left unrefrigerated for too long. Refrigeration suspends fermentation (and therefore carbonation), but it will start again when the bottles are removed from refrigeration.

It's best to bottle sodas in used (cleaned!) plastic soda bottles since it's easy to gauge carbonation just by pressing the side. Always open sodas over a sink or outside, and unscrew the cap extremely slowly to allow the pressure to release.

3 • Working in batches, puree the cherries with their liquid in a food processor or blender. Strain the puree into a bowl, collecting as much juice as possible without forcing any solids through the strainer.

4 • Pour the cherry juice into a clean 2-liter bottle using a funnel. Top off the bottle with water, leaving at least 1 inch of headspace. Give it a taste and add more lime juice or sugar, if desired. The extra sugar will dissolve on its own.

5 • Add the yeast. Screw on the cap and shake the bottle to dissolve and distribute the yeast. Let the bottle sit at room temperature out of direct sunlight until carbonated, typically 12 to 48 hours, depending on the temperature of the room. Check the bottle periodically; when it feels rock solid with very little give, it's ready.

6 • Refrigerate overnight or for up to 2 weeks. Open very slowly over a sink to release the pressure gradually and avoid bubble-ups.

HOW TO TRANSFER YOUR SODAS INTO A PRETTY BOTTLE

Pretty bottles might not be the best for making sodas, but we can certainly transfer a soda into one! Insert a small funnel into the neck of your pretty bottle and slip a chopstick inside. Holding the chopstick at an angle so that its tip touches the side of the bottle, pour your soda into the bottle. The chopstick will help minimize foaming as the soda is poured. Be sure to drink all the soda you transfer or transfer it back into the original bottle for safekeeping.

Grape Soda

MAKES ABOUT 8 CUPS
(ENOUGH TO FILL A 2-LITER PLASTIC SODA BOTTLE)

I'll never forget the first time I casually popped a Concord grape in my mouth while wandering through a California farmers' market. I may have gasped. I definitely swooned. If you've never had one, a Concord grape tastes like child-hood: sugary grape soda, grape jelly sand-wiches, grape popsicles—the purest, most authentic grape you can imagine. It's worth seeking out real Concord grapes or 100 percent Concord grape juice for this recipe. For a lighter champagnelike soda, try making it with red or green table grapes.

4 pounds Concord grapes, or 6 cups Concord grape juice

½ cup freshly squeezed lemon juice (from 3 to 4 lemons), plus more if needed

1 cup water, plus more to fill the bottles

14 tablespoons / 6 ounces white granulated sugar, plus more if needed

Pinch of salt

⅛ teaspoon dry champagne yeast

1 • Pulse the grapes a few times in a food processor or blender to break them into big chunks. Don't bother removing the grape seeds. Combine the fruit with the lemon juice in a large bowl.

2 • Bring the water to a boil in a small saucepan on the stove top or in the micro-wave. Remove from the heat. Add the sugar and salt, stir to dissolve, and pour over the grapes. Let this stand for 10 minutes to mac-erate the fruit. If using grape juice, simply combine the juice with the liquid and skip to the bottling step.

3 • Working in batches, puree the grapes with their liquid in a food processor or blender. Strain the puree into a bowl, col-lecting as much juice as possible without forcing any solids through the strainer.

4 • Pour the juice into the clean 2-liter bottle using the funnel. Top off the bottle with water, leaving at least 1 inch of headspace. Give it a taste and add more lemon juice or sugar, if desired. The extra sugar will dis-solve on its own.

5 • Add the yeast. Screw on the cap and shake the bottle to dissolve and distribute the yeast. Let the bottle sit at room tempera-ture out of direct sunlight until carbonated, typically 12 to 48 hours, depending on the temperature of the room. Check the bottle periodically; when it feels rock solid with very little give, it's ready.

6 • Refrigerate overnight or for up to 2 weeks. Open very slowly over a sink to release the pressure gradually and avoid bubble-ups.

Grapefruit Soda

MAKES ABOUT 8 CUPS
(ENOUGH TO FILL A 2-LITER PLASTIC SODA BOTTLE)

Here's one for the folks in our listening audience who prefer tart to sweet and request water over the offer of other, more sugary beverages (I'm looking at you, Dad). This grapefruit soda is austere in its ingredients but sings in the mouth. It's sour and sparkling, and solidly grown-up. Speaking of which, try it with gin—you won't be sorry.

1 cup water, plus more to fill the bottles

9 tablespoons / 4 ounces white granulated sugar, plus more if needed

Pinch of salt

4 cups grapefruit juice (from 6 to 7 large grapefruits)

⅛ teaspoon dry champagne yeast

1 • Bring the water to a boil in a small saucepan on the stove top or in the microwave. Remove from the heat. Add the sugar and salt and stir to dissolve. Cool and combine with grapefruit juice.

2 • Pour the juice into a clean 2-liter bottle using a funnel. Top off the bottle with water, leaving at least 1 inch of headspace. Give it a taste and add more sugar, if desired. The extra sugar will dissolve on its own.

3 • Add the yeast. Screw on the cap and shake the bottle to dissolve and distribute the yeast. Let the bottle sit at room temperature out of direct sunlight until carbonated, typically 12 to 48 hours, depending on the temperature of the room. Check the bottle periodically; when it feels rock solid with very little give, it's ready.

4 • Refrigerate overnight or for up to 2 weeks. Open very slowly over a sink to release the pressure gradually and avoid bubble-ups.

Root Beer

MAKES ABOUT 8 CUPS
(ENOUGH TO FILL A 2-LITER PLASTIC SODA BOTTLE)

Root beer is tricky. True root beer is made with sassafras root, which is not only hard to find outside its growing region but also cannot be sold commercially. Sassafras contains a chemical, safrole, which was found to cause cancer in lab rats if consumed in large enough quantities and was subsequently banned by the FDA. You'd have to drink root beer like water to be at risk, but still. Bummer. I tried many different combinations of herbs, barks, roots, and spices to mimic an all-natural root beer at home, but at the end of the day, you really need that sassafras root. Therefore, this is one recipe where I endorse the use of syrup to get the flavor just right. I particularly like Fermentap #1 Root Beer Syrup, but any you find will make a fine soda. Since different syrups can vary in sweetness, use less sugar to start and add more to taste.

2 cups water, plus more to fill the bottles

½ to 1 cup packed / 4 to 8 ounces dark brown sugar

2½ teaspoons root beer extract

1 teaspoon vanilla extract

¼ cup / 1⅓ ounces raisins, coarsely chopped

1 star anise

Pinch of salt

⅛ teaspoon dry champagne yeast

1 • Bring the water to a simmer and remove from the heat. Add ½ cup of the brown sugar, the root beer extract, vanilla, raisins, star anise, and salt, stirring to dissolve the brown sugar. Let stand until cool.

2 • Strain the root beer syrup into a bowl and pour into a clean 2-liter bottle using a funnel. Top off the bottle with water, leaving at least 1 inch of headspace. Give it a taste and add more brown sugar, if desired. The extra sugar will dissolve on its own.

3 • Add the yeast. Screw on the cap and shake the bottle to dissolve and distribute the yeast. Let the bottle sit at room temperature out of direct sunlight until carbonated, typically 12 to 48 hours, depending on the temperature of the room. Check the bottle periodically; when it feels rock solid with very little give, it's ready.

4 • Refrigerate overnight or for up to 2 weeks. Open very slowly over a sink to release the pressure gradually and avoid bubble-ups.

CHAPTER 2

Kombucha

EXPERT INTERVIEW

Eric Childs, founder, owner, and kombucha brewer at Kombucha Brooklyn, Brooklyn, New York

How did you get hooked on brewing kombucha?

Like most people who have tried kombucha, I first tasted a store-bought kind. I was a very loyal and happy customer for many years. Then six or seven years ago, I found that the quality and flavor weren't as good as they used to be, so I started making it at home. I ordered a culture online, started brewing it, and gave it to my friends. They were already calling me Kombucha Man at that point. After brewing it for about a year, I saw about eight people drinking kombucha at once on the subway, and it was all a mass-produced store-bought brand. I thought, "I'm going to bring the people some local kombucha."

What is the scoby?

Scoby stands for "symbiotic culture of bacteria and yeast." Essentially, it's a patty of cellulose that is made by the bacteria during fermentation. That patty contains all the life that is in kombucha, the yeast and bacteria together.

What do you say to people who are weirded out by the scoby culture?

It *is* weird! We're not used to things growing on top of our food. There needs to be a reeducation when it comes to kombucha.

I always tell people that fermentation has been around for a very long time and in environments that were even dirtier than our own. This way of making food has been around a lot longer than our pasteurization systems. But there's no way around it: The scoby *is* weird.

What is the trickiest part of brewing kombucha?

Once you get the base down, brewing kombucha is very easy. The culture does all the work. One of the trickiest things is for people to just know their culture. Know how to culture in different environments, different temperatures, with different ingredients, and what affects the way the culture works.

What is one thing homebrewers could do to improve their kombucha?

I preach a method of keeping the tea base for the kombucha the same every time. Find out what teas your culture loves and make it every single time. Then when you flavor the kombucha after it's brewed, mess around with everything else. Fruits are great. Ginger and kombucha are a perfect marriage. Tweak ingredients. Source ingredients from higher-end places. The kombucha culture is very hardy and adaptable. Don't be scared.

KOMBUCHA BROOKLYN KOMBUCHAS TO TRY:
Straight Up

Master Kombucha Recipe

MAKES 1 GALLON

At its most basic, kombucha is fermented tea. Under the influence of the scoby, that strange and fascinating "symbiotic culture of bacteria and yeast," the tea loses its astringency and picks up complex fruity and spicy flavors. The finished kombucha is a tangy and gently effervescent brew that also happens to be chock full of healthy and helpful probiotics from the fermentation process.

To increase or decrease the amount of kombucha you make, maintain the basic ratio of 1 cup white granulated sugar, 8 bags black tea (or 2 tablespoons loose tea), and 2 cups starter tea per gallon batch. One scoby will ferment any size batch, though larger batches may take longer.

Note: Avoid prolonged contact between the kombucha and metal both during and after brewing. This can affect the flavor of your kombucha and weaken the scoby over time.

INGREDIENTS

14 cups water

1 cup / 7 ounces white granulated sugar

8 bags black tea, or 2 tablespoons loose black tea

2 cups starter tea from last batch of kombucha or store-bought (unpasteurized, neutral-flavored) kombucha

1 scoby per fermentation jar (page 42)

Flavoring extras: 1 to 2 cups chopped fruit, 2 to 3 cups fruit juice, ¼ cup honey, or 2 to 4 tablespoons fresh herbs or spices

EQUIPMENT

Stockpot

Measuring cups and spoons

Long-handled spoon

Large fine-mesh strainer

1-gallon canning jar, or 2 (2-quart) canning jars with one scoby for each jar if a 1-gallon jar feels too large or cumbersome

Additional 1-gallon canning jar or multiple smaller canning jars for infusing the kombucha with flavorings

Cheesecloth or paper towels

Rubber bands

2 (2-liter) soda bottles, cleaned, or 6 (16-ounce) swing-top bottles

1 • Bring the water to a boil. Remove from the heat and stir in the sugar to dissolve. Drop in the tea and allow it to steep until the water has cooled. Depending on the size of your pot, this will take a few hours. You can speed up the cooling process by placing the pot in an ice bath.

2 • Remove the tea bags or strain out the loose tea. Stir in the starter tea. This starter tea increases the acidity of the liquid, ensuring that no unwanted bacteria takes up residence in the first few days of brewing. Pour the mixture into the 1-gallon glass jar and gently place the scoby on top with clean hands. Cover the mouth of the jar with a few layers of cheesecloth or paper towels

TROUBLESHOOTING KOMBUCHA

» It is normal for the scoby to float on the top, bottom, or sideways in the jar. It is also normal for brown strings to form below the scoby or to collect on the bottom. If your scoby develops a hole, bumps, dried patches, darker brown patches, or clear jellylike patches, it is still fine to use. Usually, these are all indicative of changes in the environment of your kitchen and not a problem with the scoby itself.

» Kombucha will start off with a neutral aroma and then smell progressively more vinegary as brewing progresses. If it starts to smell cheesy, rotten, or otherwise unpleasant, this is a sign that something has gone wrong. If you see no signs of fuzzy mold on the scoby, discard the liquid only and begin again with fresh tea. If you do see signs of mold, discard both the scoby and the liquid and begin again with new ingredients.

» A scoby will last a very long time, but it's not indestructible. If the scoby becomes black, it has passed its lifespan. If it develops green or black mold, it is has become infected. In both of these cases, throw away the scoby and begin again.

» To prolong the life and maintain the health of your scoby, stick to the ratio of sugar, tea, starter tea, and water outlined in the recipe. You can also peel off the bottom (oldest) layer every few batches. This can be discarded, composted, used to start a new batch of kombucha, or given to friends to start their own.

» If you're ever in doubt about whether there is a problem with your scoby, just continue brewing batches, but discard the kombucha they make. If there's a problem, it will worsen over time and eventually become very apparent. If it's just a natural aspect of the scoby, then it will stay consistent from batch to batch, and you'll know the kombucha is fine for drinking.

secured with a rubber band. This covering allows airflow to the kombucha while keeping out dust, gnats, and other unwanted airborne particles.

3 • Keep the jar at room temperature, out of direct sunlight, and where it won't get jostled. Ferment for 7 to 10 days, checking the kombucha and the scoby periodically. It's not unusual for the scoby to float at the top, bottom, or even sideways. A new cream-colored layer of scoby should start forming on the surface of the kombucha within a few days. It usually attaches to the old scoby,

but it's okay if they separate. You may also see brown stringy bits floating beneath the scoby, sediment collecting at the bottom, and bubbles around the edges of the scoby. These are all normal signs of healthy fermentation.

4 • After 7 days, begin tasting the kombucha daily by pouring a little out of the jar and into a cup. When it reaches a balance of sweetness and tartness that is pleasant to you, the kombucha is ready to bottle.

continued

5 • Before bottling, prepare another pot of strong sugary tea for your next batch of kombucha, as outlined above.

6 • With clean hands, gently lift the scoby out of the kombucha and set it on a clean plate. As you do, check it over. It should feel thick and rubbery with a creamy layer on top and darker layers below. Some darker spots are fine, but if you see anything that looks black or moldy, discard the scoby and this batch of kombucha immediately and start over. When a mature scoby gets very thick, peel away the bottom few layers. You can either discard them or share them with a friend.

HOW TO PUT YOUR KOMBUCHA ON PAUSE

Wondering what to do with your scoby if you're heading out on vacation or just want to take a break? If you'll be gone for two weeks or less, just brew a fresh batch before you go and leave your kombucha on the counter. The kombucha may become too vinegary to drink by the end, but you can just discard it and start again with a fresh batch.

For longer breaks, make a half batch of sugar-tea and place the jar in the fridge. Replace the liquid every 4 to 6 weeks. Keep in mind that the longer the scoby is dormant, the more difficulty it will have recovering once you start brewing again.

7 • Measure out 2 cups of starter tea from this batch of kombucha and set it aside. Pour the fermented kombucha into bottles along with any juice you may want to use as flavoring. Leave at least 1 inch of headspace in each bottle. (Alternatively, infuse the kombucha with herbs, spices, or fruit for a day or two in another canning jar covered with cheesecloth, strain, and then bottle.)

8 • Store the bottled kombucha at room temperature out of direct sunlight until carbonated, typically 1 to 3 days, depending on the temperature of the room. Even if your kombucha was visibly fizzy before, this step is necessary to trap the bubbles and fully carbonate the brew. Until you get a feel for how quickly your kombucha carbonates, it's helpful to keep it in plastic bottles; the kombucha is carbonated when the bottles feel rock solid. Refrigerate to stop carbonation and then consume within a month. It is not unusual for a small "baby" scoby to form on the surface of bottled kombucha. This can be strained out while pouring.

9 • Prepare your next batch of kombucha right after bottling the previous batch. Combine the reserved starter tea with a fresh batch of sugary tea, and pour it into the cleaned fermentation jar. Slide the scoby on top, cover, and proceed with fermentation.

Peach Iced Tea Kombucha

MAKES 1 GALLON

The only thing that could possibly be better than peach iced tea on a lazy, golden-hued afternoon in late summer is fizzy peach iced tea. The combination of black and green teas gives this kombucha a softer flavor, which is better suited for showing off the juicy peaches added after fermentation. Also try adding a few tablespoons of minced ginger or replace some of the peaches with raspberries.

14 cups water

1 cup / 7 ounces white granulated sugar

5 bags black tea, or 1½ tablespoons loose
    black tea

3 bags green tea, or 1½ teaspoons loose
    green tea

2 cups starter tea from last batch of kombucha

1 scoby (page 42)

2 large peaches, diced with skins left on
    (about 2 cups)

1 • Bring the water to a boil. Remove from the heat and stir in the sugar to dissolve. Drop in the tea and allow it to steep until the water has cooled.

2 • Remove the tea bags or strain out the loose tea. Stir in the starter tea. Pour the mixture into a 1-gallon glass jar and gently place the scoby on top. Cover the mouth of the jar with a few layers of cheesecloth or paper towels secured with a rubber band.

3 • Keep the jar at room temperature, out of direct sunlight, and where it won't get jostled. Ferment for 7 to 10 days. Check the kombucha and the scoby periodically.

4 • After 7 days, begin tasting the kombucha. When it reaches a balance of sweetness and tartness that is pleasant to you, the kombucha is ready to bottle.

5 • With clean hands, gently lift the scoby out of the kombucha and set it on a clean plate. Measure out 2 cups of starter tea from this batch of kombucha and set it aside for your next.

6 • Combine the fermented kombucha and the diced peaches in a clean 1-gallon jar or divide among smaller jars. Cover the mouth of the jar with a few layers of cheesecloth or paper towels secured with a rubber band. Keep the jar at room temperature out of direct sunlight for 2 days. Strain and discard the peaches and bottle the infused kombucha. Leave at least 1 inch of headspace in the bottles.

7 • Store the bottled kombucha at room temperature out of direct sunlight until carbonated, typically 1 to 3 days, depending on the temperature of the room. Refrigerate to stop carbonation and then consume within a month.

HOW TO MAKE YOUR OWN SCOBY

If you can't find a kombucha-brewing friend from whom you can beg a scoby and you don't want to order one online, don't fret. Making your own takes some patience, but it's entirely possible.

14 cups water

1 cup / 7 ounces white granulated sugar

8 bags black tea, or 2 tablespoons loose black tea

2 cups (one 16-ounce bottle) unflavored and unpasteurized (raw) commercial kombucha

1 • Bring the water to a boil in a large pot. Remove from the heat and stir in the sugar until dissolved. Drop in the tea and allow it to steep until the water has cooled. Remove the tea bags or strain out the loose tea. Stir in the commercial kombucha. Pour the mixture into a 1-gallon glass jar or two 2-quart jars, depending on whether you want to make one scoby or two. Cover the mouth of the jar(s) with a few layers of cheesecloth or paper towels secured with a rubber band.

2 • Keep the jar(s) at room temperature, out of direct sunlight, and where it won't get jostled. Ferment for 7 to 14 days. Check the kombucha daily. You won't see much action for the first few days. Around day 5, you may start to see little groupings of white froth or bubbles on the surface. A few days later, a transparent gel should start to form over the surface of the liquid, and it will start to smell vinegary. The gel will eventually darken to a creamy beige, but may look bubbly, puckered, spotted, or otherwise primordial. This is all fine.

3 • When the scoby has formed a thick jelly layer $\frac{1}{8}$ to $\frac{1}{4}$ inch thick, it is ready to use for making kombucha. Throw away the liquid used to make the scoby and start fresh. Your first few batches of kombucha may take longer than normal or not carbonate as quickly. As the scoby becomes stronger and more adapted to the environment of your kitchen, your kombucha will become more consistent, and the scoby itself will start to look like a smooth, rubbery pancake.

Hibiscus Kombucha

MAKES 1 GALLON

Hibiscus kombucha is not what you'd expect. Where hibiscus tea tends to be rather cloying and aggressively floral, hibiscus kombucha is . . . not. In fact, it's nearly the opposite. When brewed with kombucha, hibiscus picks up some interesting berry-like flavors and sheds its saccharine character. No matter your opinion on hibiscus itself, it's worth making this kombucha just to witness the transformation.

14 cups water

1 cup / 7 ounces white granulated sugar

8 bags black tea, or 2 tablespoons loose
    black tea

2 cups starter tea from last batch of kombucha

1 scoby (page 42)

2 tablespoons dried hibiscus flowers or tea

1 • Bring the water to a boil. Remove from the heat and stir in the sugar to dissolve. Drop in the tea and allow it to steep until the water has cooled.

2 • Remove the tea bags or strain out the loose tea. Stir in the starter tea. Pour the mixture into a 1-gallon glass jar and gently place the scoby on top. Cover the mouth of the jar with a few layers of cheesecloth or paper towels secured with a rubber band.

3 • Keep the jar at room temperature, out of direct sunlight, and where it won't get jostled. Ferment for 7 to 10 days. Check the kombucha and the scoby periodically.

4 • After 7 days, begin tasting the kombucha. When it reaches a balance of sweetness and tartness that is pleasant to you, the kombucha is ready to bottle.

5 • With clean hands, gently lift the scoby out of the kombucha and set it on a clean plate. Measure out 2 cups of starter tea from this batch of kombucha and set it aside for your next.

6 • Combine the fermented kombucha and hibiscus flowers in a clean 1-gallon jar or divide among smaller jars. Cover the mouth of the jar with a few layers of cheesecloth or paper towels secured with a rubber band. Keep the jar at room temperature out of direct sunlight for 2 days. Strain the hibiscus flowers from the kombucha and bottle. Leave at least 1 inch of headspace in the bottles.

7 • Store the bottled kombucha at room temperature out of direct sunlight until carbonated, typically 1 to 3 days, depending on the temperature of the room. Refrigerate to stop carbonation and then consume within a month.

Blackberry-Sage Kombucha

MAKES 1 GALLON

Make kombucha for long enough, and you'll start playing with all sorts of things for flavoring, like whatever happens to be within eyesight when the brew is ready. This particular combination came from a handful of just-picked blackberries, a neglected bundle of sage, and a half-remembered tea I used to drink in college. Why not? As they say, necessity is the mother of awesomeness.

14 cups water

1 cup / 7 ounces white granulated sugar

8 bags black tea, or 2 tablespoons loose black tea

2 cups starter tea from last batch of kombucha

1 scoby (page 42)

14 fresh sage leaves

2 cups blackberries

1 • Bring the water to a boil. Remove from the heat and stir in the sugar to dissolve. Drop in the tea and allow it to steep until the water has cooled.

2 • Remove the tea bags or strain out the loose tea. Stir in the starter tea. Pour the mixture into a 1-gallon glass jar and gently place the scoby on top. Cover the mouth of the jar with a few layers of cheesecloth or paper towels secured with a rubber band.

3 • Keep the jar at room temperature, out of direct sunlight, and where it won't get jostled. Ferment for 7 to 10 days. Check the kombucha and the scoby periodically.

4 • After 7 days, begin tasting the kombucha. When it reaches a balance of sweetness and tartness that is pleasant to you, the kombucha is ready to bottle.

5 • With clean hands, gently lift the scoby out of the kombucha and set it on a clean plate. Measure out 2 cups of starter tea from this batch of kombucha and set it aside for your next.

6 • Tear the sage leaves into several pieces and combine with the blackberries in a clean 1-gallon jar or divide among smaller jars. Muddle with a long spoon to release the blackberry juices and bruise the leaves. Pour the kombucha over top. Cover the mouth of the jar with a few layers of cheesecloth or paper towels secured with a rubber band. Keep the jar at room temperature out of direct sunlight for 2 days. Strain the blackberries and sage leaves from the kombucha and bottle. Leave at least 1 inch of headspace in the bottles.

7 • Store the bottled kombucha at room temperature out of direct sunlight until carbonated, typically 1 to 3 days, depending on the temperature of the room. Refrigerate to stop carbonation and then consume within a month.

Honey-Green Tea Kombucha

MAKES 1 GALLON

Green tea makes an especially delicate and sophisticated kombucha. With a spot of honey to bring out the floral flavors, you could serve this at a backyard garden party from tall-stemmed glasses. Honey can be a bit hard on the scoby—its antibacterial properties can weaken the bacteria in the scoby over time. So rather than making this kombucha with the honey already in it, it's best to add it to the bottles after brewing.

14 cups water

1 cup / 7 ounces white granulated sugar

8 bags green tea, or 2 tablespoons loose green tea

2 cups starter tea from last batch of kombucha

1 scoby (page 42)

¾ cup / 9 ounces honey

1 • Bring the water to a boil. Remove from the heat and stir in the sugar to dissolve. Drop in the tea and allow it to steep until the water has cooled.

2 • Remove the tea bags or strain out the loose tea. Stir in the starter tea. Pour the mixture into a 1-gallon glass jar and gently place the scoby on top. Cover the mouth of the jar with a few layers of cheesecloth or paper towels secured with a rubber band.

3 • Keep the jar at room temperature, out of direct sunlight, and where it won't get jostled. Ferment for 7 to 10 days. Check the kombucha and the scoby periodically.

4 • After 7 days, begin tasting the kombucha. When it reaches a balance of sweetness and tartness that is pleasant to you, the kombucha is ready to bottle.

5 • With clean hands, gently lift the scoby out of the kombucha and set it on a clean plate. Measure out 2 cups of starter tea from this batch of kombucha and set it aside for your next.

6 • Divide the honey equally among the containers you are using to bottle the kombucha and pour the fermented kombucha over top. Leave at least 1 inch of headspace. Screw on the caps and shake each bottle to dissolve the honey.

7 • Store the bottled kombucha at room temperature out of direct sunlight until carbonated, typically 1 to 3 days depending on the temperature of the room. Refrigerate to stop carbonation and then consume within a month.

White Tea–Pomegranate Kombucha

MAKES 1 GALLON

The mild and fruity nature of white tea kombucha makes a nice backdrop for when you really want the flavor of a particular fruit to pop. I like pairing it with strong-tasting fruits, like pomegranate and cranberry, where the softness of the tea tempers the fruits' assertiveness without changing their essential character.

14 cups water

1 cup / 7 ounces white granulated sugar

8 bags white tea, or 2 tablespoons loose white tea

2 cups starter tea from last batch of kombucha

1 scoby (page 42)

3½ cups pomegranate juice

1 • Bring the water to a boil. Remove from heat and stir in the sugar to dissolve. Drop in the tea and allow it to steep until the water has cooled.

2 • Remove the tea bags or strain out the loose tea. Stir in the starter tea. Pour the mixture into a 1-gallon glass jar and gently place the scoby on top. Cover the mouth of the jar with a few layers of cheesecloth or paper towels secured with a rubber band.

3 • Keep the jar at room temperature, out of direct sunlight, and where it won't get jostled. Ferment for 7 to 10 days. Check the kombucha and the scoby periodically.

4 • After 7 days, begin tasting the kombucha. When it reaches a balance of sweetness and tartness that is pleasant to you, the kombucha is ready to bottle.

5 • With clean hands, gently lift the scoby out of the kombucha and set it on a clean plate. Measure out your 2 cups of starter tea from this batch of kombucha and set it aside for your next.

6 • Combine the fermented kombucha and pomegranate juice in a clean pitcher. Pour into bottles, leaving at least 1 inch of headspace.

7 • Store the bottled kombucha at room temperature out of direct sunlight until carbonated, typically 1 to 3 days, depending on the temperature of the room. Refrigerate to stop carbonation and then consume within a month.

OTHER WAYS TO FLAVOR YOUR KOMBUCHA

Always stick to the same ratio of ingredients as described in the Master Kombucha Recipe (page 38). But beyond that, it's play time.

Black tea tends to be the easiest type of tea for the scoby to ferment. But once your scoby is going strong, you can try branching out into other kinds of tea. Green tea, white tea, oolong tea, or a combination of these make especially good kombucha. Herbal teas are okay, but use at least a few bags of caffeinated black tea in the mix to be sure the scoby is getting all the nutrients it needs (finished kombucha does contain some caffeine). Avoid any teas that contain oils, like Earl Grey or flavored teas.

For the sugar, plain old white granulated sugar (preferably organic) is the easiest for the yeasts and bacteria in the scoby to consume. Other sugars such as brown sugar, turbinado, and honey should be used with caution because they are tougher to digest and can disrupt the ecosystem of the scoby. If used, keep a close eye on the scoby and go back to white sugar every few batches. For the health of the scoby, always maintain the ratio of sugar to water from the master recipe. Reduced-sugar kombuchas are not recommended. However, the longer you let your kombucha ferment, the more sugar is consumed and the less is left in the finished brew.

For flavoring a 1-gallon batch of kombucha after brewing, try adding any of the following: 2 cups diced fruit, 2 to 3 cups of fruit juice, several tablespoons of minced ginger, several tablespoons of another flavored tea, or fresh herbs and spices.

CHAPTER 3

Kefir

EXPERT INTERVIEW

Nancy Van Brasch Hamren, originator and namesake of Nancy's Yogurt, Eugene, Oregon

How did you get hooked on making kefir?

We started making kefir within two or three years of opening Nancy's Yogurt in the early '70s. We used a mix of cultures for it at first and sweetened it with honey. It had a loyal but small following for years. Four years ago, we decided we needed to either remodel the kefir or get rid of it. So we got better cartons, went totally organic, and flavored it with organic agave and organic fruits.

Why should people drink kefir?

Things that are fermented are easier to digest. When you add bacteria or yeast to milk, they break down the casein and lactose, digest it, and produce lactic acid and B vitamins. Some people have trouble drinking milk but are just fine eating yogurt or kefir. Fermenting it makes the food more available for the body to digest.

How would you describe its flavor?

It's a tangy cross between buttermilk and yogurt. One of the flavor compounds is acetaldehyde, which is the characteristic green-apple flavor produced by the kefir culture. Another is lactic acid, which is like the flavor of buttermilk. And then the third is diacetyl, which is the buttery smell and flavor. There's also a little acetic acid, which is vinegary.

What is the trickiest part of making kefir?

The difficult part is really how much you want to invest to make the product right. Our kefir is made in a vat. When it reaches the right acidity and thickness, then we start cooling it down really, really slowly. You can make a knock-off version of all that by skipping steps or adding other ingredients to duplicate the thickness and flavor. But it's not really fermented; the lactose isn't really broken down.

What is one thing homebrewers could do to improve their kefir?

I love the idea of people playing with their food. Don't be afraid, just goof around and see what works. Play with the variables until you get it where you want it to be. Kefir grains are mesophilic, meaning they have designed themselves to grow at room temperature. A few tablespoons of powdered milk will also increase the solids and help the bacteria and yeast grow because that's what they feed on.

NANCY'S YOGURT KEFIRS TO TRY: raspberry, peach

Master Milk Kefir Recipe

MAKES 1 CUP

Think of kefir as liquid yogurt. It's thicker than milk but not quite as spoonable as yogurt, though it tastes nearly identical. Kefir also has all the same healthy bacteria and probiotics as yogurt, with the added bonus of some yeast. This is all thanks to a few teensy little kefir grains, which will work tirelessly, batch after batch, to culture your milk. It should be noted that kefir grains do not actually contain any grain and are gluten free. Like the kombucha scoby, they are naturally occurring cellular structures of bacteria and yeast.

To increase the amount of kefir you make with each batch, just maintain the ratio of 1 cup milk to 1 teaspoon grains. After some time, your grains will start to multiply. You can split them to brew separate simultaneous batches of kefir, give them to a friend, or dry them for longer storage (see How to Put Your Milk or Water Kefir on Pause, page 59).

Note: Avoid prolonged contact between the kefir grains or the kefir and metal both during and after fermentation. This can affect the flavor of your kefir and weaken the grains over time.

INGREDIENTS
1 cup milk (see Brewer's Pantry, page 4)
1 teaspoon kefir grains

EQUIPMENT
1-pint canning jar
Measuring cups and spoons
Long-handled spoon
Cheesecloth or paper towels
Rubber band
Small fine-mesh strainer
Glass or plastic lidded container

1 • Pour the milk into the glass jar and stir in the kefir grains. Cover the jar with a few layers of cheesecloth or paper towels and secure with a rubber band.

2 • Store the jar at room temperature out of direct sunlight and allow it to ferment until thickened. Healthy kefir grains at around 70°F will typically culture in 24 hours, though it may culture in as little as 12 hours at warm temperatures, or take as long as 48 hours at cooler temperatures. Check the kefir periodically until you have a sense of how quickly it is fermenting. (See Troubleshooting Milk Kefir, page 54.)

3 • Strain the kefir into a glass or plastic storage container, stirring gently until just the grains are left in the strainer. Refrigerate the kefir in a sealed container and use within 2 weeks. Stir your grains into a new jar of milk to make another batch of kefir.

continued

Straining the grains from the kefir

TROUBLESHOOTING MILK KEFIR

» If your kefir separates with a thick layer on top and a watery layer on bottom, this is a sign that the kefir has overfermented. The grains are still healthy and the kefir is fine to eat, but try culturing the subsequent batches for less time.

» If your kefir hasn't cultured within 48 hours, strain the kefir and begin again with fresh milk. Depending on the circumstances (a cold room, reviving dehydrated kefir grains, a new kind of milk, etc.), it may take several batches before the kefir begins culturing normally.

» At temperatures above 90°F, the milk tends to sour or grow harmful bacteria faster than the kefir can do its job, eventually killing the kefir itself. If the temperature of your home becomes very hot during the summer, find a cooler spot to store your kefir or store it in the refrigerator during the hottest days.

» If at any time the milk or the kefir itself starts to smell or look unappetizing, immediately strain out the kefir grains, discard the milk, and begin with a new batch. If this happens several times in a row, your grains have likely died and you'll need to begin again with new grains.

Master Water Kefir Recipe

MAKES 4 CUPS

Where milk kefir thrives on the lactose in milk, water kefir grains live on sugar dissolved in water. On its own, brewed water kefir tastes blandly sweet—it needs a squeeze of lemon and a cup or two of chopped fruit to make our mouths happy. Let the flavored kefir carbonate for a few days, and by golly, it could pass for soda with none the wiser. Water kefir is also gluten free and full of healthful probiotics.

To increase the amount of kefir you make with each batch, just maintain the ratio of 4 cups of sugar water to at least 1 tablespoon of grains. After some time, your grains will start to multiply. You can split them to brew separate simultaneous batches of water kefir, give them to a friend, or dry them for longer storage (see How to Put Your Milk or Water Kefir on Pause, page 59).

Note: Avoid prolonged contact between the kefir grains or the kefir and metal both during and after fermentation. This can affect the flavor of your kefir and weaken the grains over time.

INGREDIENTS

4 cups water

4½ tablespoons / 2 ounces white granulated sugar (for lighter-tasting kefir) or turbinado sugar (for stronger-tasting kefir)

1 to 3 tablespoons water kefir grains

Juice from 1 lemon

Flavoring extras: ½ to 1 cup diced fruit or fruit juice

EQUIPMENT

1-quart canning jar

Measuring cups and spoons

Long-handled spoon

Cheesecloth or paper towels

Rubber band

Small fine-mesh strainer

1 (1-liter) soda bottle, cleaned, or 2 (16-ounce) swing-top bottles

1 • Bring the water to a boil. Remove the pan from the heat, add the sugar, and stir to dissolve. Set the pan aside until the water has completely cooled. This will take an hour or two, or you can speed up the cooling process by placing the pot in an ice bath.

2 • Pour the sugar water into the glass jar. Add the kefir grains and cover the mouth of the jar with a few layers of cheesecloth or paper towels secured with a rubber band. Store the jar at room temperature out of direct sunlight and allow it to ferment for 48 hours.

3 • During this time, you may not see much activity from the kefir. A few bubbles may form on the surface and the water may become cloudy, but don't worry if you don't see these things. The finished kefir will taste sweet, but less so than at the start of fermentation. The best indication that the water kefir is fermenting properly is if it carbonates in the next step.

continued

MASTER WATER KEFIR RECIPE, CONTINUED

4 • Strain the water kefir into a measuring cup and stir in the lemon juice. Transfer the prepared kefir into bottles along with any juice you may want to use as flavoring. Leave at least 1 inch of headspace in each bottle. (Alternatively, infuse the kefir with herbs, spices, or fruit for a day or two in another canning jar covered with cheesecloth, strain, and then bottle.) Stir the grains into a new jar of sugar water to start another batch of kefir.

5 • Store the bottled kefir at room temperature out of direct sunlight until carbonated, typically 1 to 3 days. Exact fermentation time will depend on the temperature in the room: water kefir will carbonate quickly at warm temperatures and take longer at cooler temperatures. Even if your water kefir was visibly fizzy before, this step is necessary to trap the bubbles and fully carbonate the brew. Until you get a feel for how quickly your kefir carbonates, it's helpful to keep it in plastic bottles; the kefir is carbonated when the bottles feel rock solid.

6 • Refrigerate to stop carbonation and then consume within a month.

TROUBLESHOOTING WATER KEFIR

» Water kefir grains work best at an average room temperature of 70°F. If it is colder in your home, the grains may take longer to work. If it is warmer, they may culture the sugar water more quickly.

» Water kefir grains are very resilient little things. If you forgot to dechlorinate your water or left the last batch on the counter for too long, they may behave sluggishly for a few days, but they'll spring back. A new batch of dehydrated grains may take a few rounds to rehydrate and begin culturing properly.

» Also try switching to organic sugar if you haven't been using it already. Regular nonorganic sugar can contain chemicals that weaken the grains over time.

» If you've accounted for all of these things, but your water kefir grains are being listless, smell overly yeasty or cheesy, feel slimy, or just seem off to you, try giving them a little R&R in a batch of Water Kefir Recovery Brew (page 65).

Cherry, Pistachio, and Cardamom Kefir Smoothie

SERVES 1

While it might be a long shot to expect cherries, pistachios, and cardamom on a deserted island, this is what I would want on mine. The combination of these three friends never gets old for me, plus the pistachios give the smoothie an extra-thick texture. I will have to hope that my island also comes equipped with a functioning blender.

1 cup milk kefir (page 53)
1 cup fresh or frozen pitted sweet cherries
1 tablespoon honey
¼ teaspoon ground cardamom
2 tablespoons shelled pistachios

• Combine all of the ingredients in a blender. Blend on high speed until smooth and creamy.

Banana-Berry Kefir Smoothie

SERVES 1

This is my go-to "make it and get out the door" smoothie. I like the balance of tart strawberries and sweet blueberries, and the banana makes it taste almost like ice cream. With one of these smoothies in my belly, I have enough energy for whatever the morning has to throw at me.

1 cup milk kefir (page 53)
½ ripe banana, sliced
¼ cup fresh or frozen strawberries
¼ cup fresh or frozen blueberries
2 tablespoons maple syrup
½ teaspoon ground cinnamon
Pinch of ground nutmeg

• Combine all of the ingredients in a blender. Blend on high speed until smooth and creamy.

Mango Lassi Kefir Smoothie

SERVES 1

The hotter and more sticky-humid the day, the more desirable a mango lassi becomes. I'm pretty sure they're genetically engineered that way. Not only does it hit the spot for something both sweet and a little sour, it also serves as a meal on those days when heat chases away your appetite.

1 cup milk kefir (page 53)

1 very ripe mango, peeled and coarsely chopped, or 1 cup frozen mango

1 tablespoon honey

• Combine all of the ingredients in a blender. Blend on high speed until smooth and creamy.

HOW TO PUT YOUR MILK OR WATER KEFIR ON PAUSE

To take a break from making kefir, just transfer the grains into a fresh batch of milk or sugar water and place the jar in the fridge. The yeast and bacteria in the grains will go dormant in the cold and can be kept this way for up to a month. Kefir grains just coming out of dormancy might take a few batches to begin fully culturing again. Switch out the old milk or sugar water for new liquids every 48 hours until you begin to see signs of fermentation (thickening of the milk kefir and less-sweet-tasting water kefir).

For longer storage, or if your grains have multiplied and you have extra, you can dry your kefir grains. Rinse them in dechlorinated water and lay the grains on a piece of parchment paper somewhere out of the way. They will dry within a few days and can be stored in the fridge for up to a year. To reactivate, begin brewing as usual but expect them to take a few batches before fully culturing again.

Ginger-Pear Kefir

MAKES 4 CUPS

This may seem like a lot of pear for the amount of kefir. And it is. Pear has such a delicate flavor that you have to overdo it a bit just to get it to show up to the party. Ginger is the supporting actor in this scenario, adding a spicy backbone to pear's shy charm.

4 cups water kefir (page 55)
2 tablespoons freshly squeezed lemon juice (from 1 lemon)
2 ripe pears, skins left on, cored, and diced (roughly 2 cups)
1-inch piece gingerroot, peeled and minced

1 • Combine all of the ingredients in a 2-quart canning jar (or divide between smaller canning jars) and cover with a piece of cheesecloth or paper towel secured with a rubber band. Keep the jar at room temperature out of direct sunlight for 2 days. Strain and discard the pear and ginger pieces and bottle the infused kefir.

2 • Store the bottled kefir at room temperature out of direct sunlight until carbonated, typically 1 to 3 days, depending on the temperature of the room. Refrigerate to stop carbonation and then consume within a month.

Coconut Water Kefir

MAKES 4 CUPS

Kefir grains love coconut water. They go crazy for the stuff. You can almost see them rubbing their bellies as they settle into the jar. Unfortunately, coconut water for kefir grains is a bit like an ice cream binge for humans. To keep the grains healthy and happy, switch back to the sugar-water solution every few batches to make sure they're getting all the nutrients they need.

4 cups coconut water
1 tablespoon water kefir grains

1 • Pour the coconut water into a 1-quart canning jar. Add the kefir grains and cover with a few layers of cheesecloth or paper towels secured with a rubber band. Store the jar at room temperature out of direct sunlight and allow it to ferment for 24 to 48 hours. Coconut water kefir may ferment more quickly than other kefirs, so check it frequently after the first 12 hours and proceed when the kefir tastes good to you. Overfermented coconut water kefir will start to taste sour.

2 • Strain the coconut water kefir into a measuring cup, and then transfer to bottles along with any juice, herbs, or fruit you may want to use as flavoring. Leave at least 1 inch of headspace in each bottle.

3 • Store the bottled kefir at room temperature out of direct sunlight until carbonated, typically 1 to 3 days, depending on the temperature of the room. Refrigerate to stop carbonation and then consume within a month.

Sparkling Raspberry Kefir Wine

MAKES 8 CUPS
TARGET ORIGINAL GRAVITY RANGE = 1.045–1.050
TARGET FINAL GRAVITY RANGE = 1.000–1.001
TARGET ABV = 7 PERCENT

If you want your probiotics and your evening tipple all in one, look no further. Yes, indeed, kefir grains can be used to make wine. You just need to give them enough sugar and then enough time to eat all the sugar. And by the way, I happen to know that this sparkling raspberry kefir wine makes an especially good sangria base. (For a more in-depth description of wine-making, see chapter 8, page 155.)

This recipe can put quite a strain on the grains, and they sometimes have trouble bouncing back. For this reason, wait to make this one until after your water kefir grains have started multiplying and then keep a few tablespoons of grains in reserve.

INGREDIENTS

8 cups water

1⅛ cups / 8 ounces white granulated sugar or turbinado sugar

1½ pounds fresh or frozen raspberries

¼ cup freshly squeezed lemon juice (from 2 lemons)

¼ teaspoon tannin (optional, if a dry wine is desired; see Brewer's Pantry, page 7)

2 tablespoons water kefir grains

1 cup / 1 ounce Splenda or other nonfermentable sugar (optional)

3 tablespoons / 1 ounce corn sugar dissolved in ½ cup boiling water and cooled, for bottling

EQUIPMENT

Stockpot

Measuring cups and spoons

Long-handled spoon

Cheesecloth

1-gallon jug

Hydrometer

Stopper

Air lock

Strainer

Racking cane and tip

Siphon hose

Hose clamp

Bottle filler

5 (12-ounce) beer bottles

Bottle caps

1 • Bring the water to a boil. Remove the pan from the heat, add the sugar and the raspberries, and stir to dissolve the sugar. Set the pan aside until the water has completely cooled. This will take an hour or two.

continued

SPARKLING RASPBERRY KEFIR WINE, CONTINUED

2 • Sanitize a 1-gallon jug, stopper, and air lock (see page 14).

3 • Pour the sugar water and raspberries into the jug. Add the lemon juice and tannin (if using), and shake the jug to mix everything together and aerate the liquid. Take a hydrometer reading to determine the original gravity (see Brewer's Handbook, page 16). Tie the kefir grains in a piece of cheesecloth and add them to the jug. Insert the stopper into the neck of the jug. Fill the air lock and insert it into the stopper.

4 • Store the jug at room temperature out of direct sunlight and allow it to ferment for 2 weeks. Gently shake the jug daily to mix the ingredients. Fermentation should become active within a few days, peak around a week, and slowly taper off in the second week.

5 • After 2 weeks, sanitize a stockpot and a strainer, and strain the kefir wine into the stockpot. Clean and sanitize the jug, stopper, and air lock. Transfer the kefir wine back to the jug and reattach the stopper and air lock. Store at room temperature out of direct sunlight for 2 weeks to allow time for all of the sediment created during fermentation to settle out. Place the strained kefir grains in a batch of Water Kefir Recovery Brew (page 65).

6 • Sanitize a stockpot, a long-handled spoon, a hydrometer, racking cane and tip, siphon hose, hose clamp, bottle filler, five 12-ounce beer bottles or plastic bottles, and bottle caps. Siphon $1/2$ cup of the kefir wine to the hydrometer and use to determine the final gravity. Drink the wine or pour it back into the jug once used.

7 • Pour the corn sugar solution into the stockpot. Siphon the kefir wine into the stockpot to mix with the corn sugar solution, splashing as little as possible. Scoop a little wine with the measuring cup and give it a taste. Add Splenda (or other back-sweetener, see page 71) if a sweeter wine is desired. Siphon the kefir wine into bottles, cap, and label.

8 • Let the bottles sit at room temperature out of direct sunlight for 2 weeks to fully carbonate. Store for up to a year. Refrigerate before serving.

KEFIR

WATER KEFIR RECOVERY BREW

This recipe, adapted from one used by Cultures for Health (see Resources, page 176), gives weary kefir grains an extra-large dose of all the essential nutrients, minerals, and vitamins they like best. Refrigerating the grains also makes them go dormant, giving them a break from the tough job of fermenting our brews. Grains will come back from their break healthier and ready to go.

5 cups water

¼ cup / 2 ounces turbinado sugar

⅛ teaspoon coarse-grain sea salt, such as Maldon

¼ teaspoon baking soda

½ teaspoon molasses

1 • Bring the water to a boil. Remove the pan from heat and scoop out 1 cup of water to set aside. Add the sugar, sea salt, baking soda, and molasses to the remaining water, and stir to dissolve. Let the water cool completely.

2 • Strain the kefir grains from their current batch of kefir as normal. While still in the strainer, rinse them a few times with the reserved cup of water. Combine the rinsed grains and the Recovery Brew in a glass jar, cover with plastic wrap secured with a rubber band, and place in the fridge for at least 1 week, or up to 4 weeks. (The plastic wrap will allow trapped gasses to escape while also protecting the liquid.)

3 • To begin brewing again, strain the grains and discard the Recovery Brew. Transfer the grains into a fresh batch of sugar water to culture.

Hard Cider

EXPERT INTERVIEW

Jeffrey House, owner of ACE Cider, Sebastopol, California

How did you get hooked on fermenting cider?

I first came to the U.S. to export California wine and import British ales. I did that for a number of years before coming to Sebastopol and seeing all the apple trees. This area of Sonoma was like England with sun! Turns out this area of California was the number-one area for growing apples. I thought there must be cideries around, but they were just growing apples for apple juice or applesauce. No one was making cider! I thought, "You guys are missing the boat." We had one guy make us cider, and it was rubbish. So we tried it ourselves and the rest is history.

What makes a truly stellar cider?

I like balance. You want a certain sweetness, a certain aroma, and a nice crisp finish. Here, we use a balance of apples: Gravensteins in July and then Romes and Jonathans in the fall. You can get astringency from Granny Smith–type apples and sweetness from Fuji or dessert apples. We look for certain sugars and certain acids in the fruit.

What is the trickiest part of cider-making?

The biggest problem with cider-making is the apples. If you don't put good fruit in, you won't get good cider out. We ferment as much as we can during the season, and then we keep apples in cold storage and bring those out on occasion. We're basically making a new batch every week, and we don't really stop.

Where do you get inspiration for new ciders?

We just try new things. Right now we have a few barrels of traditional British cider going. I also just read about someone using beer yeast to make ciders, which is interesting since the yeast is usually what decides how the cider tastes. The next phase is to make cider from one particular variety. We're interested in using Orange Pippins.

What is one thing homebrewers could do to improve their ciders?

Experiment and see what you like. I think sometimes homebrewers make ciders too strong. They don't cut off the fermentation; they want it bone dry and then it finishes up very strong. We called that scrumpy in England!

CIDERS TO TRY: apple, Joker, perry, berry, and pumpkin

Master Hard Cider Recipe

MAKES 1 GALLON

While a crisp and sparkling apple cider made with fresh-pressed local apples is certainly a thing of beauty, why limit ourselves to ciders with just one fruit? In my kitchen, a cider is very loosely defined as anything brewed primarily with fruit juice (instead of whole fruit pieces) while being typically lighter in body and less alcoholic than wine. Any fruit. Any juice. I recommend trying them all.

Your fruit juice and taste preferences can be your guide for adding the other ingredients in this recipe. Most fruit juices have enough natural sugars to give the yeast something to eat, but you can add more if you'd like to bump up the alcohol content. The sugar won't sweeten the cider in this case; for a sweet cider, you'll need to back-sweeten before bottling (see Back-Sweetening, page 71).

Add acid blend to balance out fruits with little natural acidity. Ditto with adding tannin. Err on the side of caution to begin with since you can always add more of these ingredients once you taste the cider before bottling. Use a second Campden tablet just before bottling to make a still (nonsparkling) cider. For a sparkling cider, skip the second Campden and add a little corn sugar during bottling to carbonate.

One last note: Cider tends to have a funky aroma when first fermented, which fades after some time in the bottle. For this reason, it's best to wait at least a month before cracking open your ciders.

INGREDIENTS

- 1 gallon fruit juice (100 percent juice, no added sugar, and preferably unpasteurized)
- 1⅛ to 2¼ cups / 8 to 16 ounces white granulated sugar, honey, or other fermentable sugar (optional)
- 1 to 2 Campden tablets
- 2 teaspoons (1 packet) dry wine or beer yeast, or 1½ tablespoons (½ tube) liquid cider or beer yeast
- 1 teaspoon yeast nutrient
- ½ teaspoon pectic enzyme
- 1 to 2 teaspoons acid blend (optional)
- ⅛ to ¼ teaspoon tannin (optional)
- 1 cup / 1 ounce Splenda or other nonfermentable sugar (optional; see Back-Sweetening, page 71)
- 3 tablespoons / 1 ounce corn sugar dissolved in ½ cup boiling water and cooled (optional, for bottling)

EQUIPMENT

Stockpot

Measuring cups and spoons

Long-handled spoon

Hydrometer

2-gallon fermentation bucket with lid

Air lock

1-quart canning jar

1-gallon jug

Stopper

Racking cane and tip

Siphon hose

Hose clamp

Bottle filler

10 (12-ounce) beer bottles or 6 (22-ounce) beer bottles

Bottle caps

Bottle capper

Optional bottling alternative for nonsparkling ciders: 5 (750-milliliter) wine bottles with corks and a wine corker

1 • Sanitize a 2-gallon bucket, its lid, the air lock, and a spoon for stirring.

2 • If using a fermentable sugar, bring the fruit juice to a simmer in a stockpot, remove from the heat, and stir in the sugar to dissolve. Cool to room temperature.

3 • Pour the fruit juice into the 2-gallon fermentation bucket. Take a hydrometer reading to determine the original gravity (see Brewer's Handbook, page 16). Crush 1 Campden tablet and stir it into the juice. Snap on the lid and attach the air lock. Wait 24 hours for the Campden to sterilize the juice. (If you are using pasteurized fruit juice, you can skip this sterilizing step.)

4 • After the juice is sterilized, prepare the yeast starter. Sanitize a measuring cup, a 1-quart canning jar, and a long-handled spoon. Scoop out 1 cup juice and pour it into the jar. Sprinkle the yeast over top and cover the jar with a piece of plastic wrap secured with a rubber band. Give the jar a good shake and let it stand for 1 to 3 hours. Dry yeast will get very bubbly and foamy; liquid yeast gets less foamy but you will see tiny bubbles popping on the surface of the liquid if you look closely. Once you see some sign of activity, the yeast starter is ready to be used. (See Brewer's Handbook, page 15.)

5 • Pour the starter into the juice along with the yeast nutrient and pectic enzyme. If using acid blend and tannin, start with lesser amounts; you can add more before bottling, if needed. Stir vigorously to distribute the yeast and aerate the juice. Snap the lid back on and reattach the air lock. You should see active fermentation as evidenced by bubbles in the air lock within 48 hours.

6 • Let the cider ferment undisturbed for at least 3 days or up to 7 days, until fermentation has slowed and the sediment created during brewing has had a chance to settle. At this point, the cider is ready to be transferred off the sediment and into a smaller 1-gallon jug for the longer secondary fermentation.

continued

MASTER HARD CIDER RECIPE, CONTINUED

7 • Sanitize a 1-gallon jug, its stopper, the racking cane, its tip, the siphon hose, and the hose clamp. Siphon all of the cider into the jug. Tilt the bucket toward the end to siphon all of the liquid. Stop when you see the liquid in the hose becoming cloudy with sediment. (See Brewer's Handbook, page 16.)

8 • Seal the jug with its stopper and insert the air lock. Let it sit somewhere cool and dark for another 2 weeks. By this point, you should see no real signs of fermentation. Watch the air lock: If 2 minutes pass without seeing any bubbles, fermentation is essentially complete. If you do see a bubble, let it sit for another several days until you no longer see any bubbles.

9 • Before bottling, taste the cider and make adjustments as needed. Add Splenda (or other back-sweetener, see page 71) if a sweeter cider is desired. If it tastes too sweet, you can add extra acid blend to give it some tartness and/or some tannin to give dryness and astringency. If adding tannin, let the cider sit for another week or two for the flavor to develop and taste again before bottling.

10 • If a nonsparkling cider is desired, crush a second Campden tablet, add it to the jug of cider, and wait 24 hours before bottling.

11 • To bottle the cider, sanitize a stockpot, a hydrometer, ten 12-ounce beer bottles or six 22-ounce beer bottles, their caps, the siphon hose, the racking cane, its tip, a measuring cup, and the bottle filler. Siphon ½ cup of cider to the hydrometer and use to determine final gravity. Drink the cider or pour it back into the jug once used.

12 • For nonsparkling cider, siphon into bottles, cap, and label. To make a sparkling cider, pour the corn sugar solution into the stockpot. Siphon the cider into the stockpot to mix with the corn sugar solution, splashing as little as possible. Siphon the cider into bottles, cap, and label.

13 • Store bottles of sparkling or nonsparkling cider in a cool, dark place for at least 1 month or up to 1 year. Sparkling cider is usually served chilled. Nonsparkling cider can be served chilled or at room temperature.

BACK-SWEETENING: WHEN, WHY, AND HOW

You run into a problem with lower-alcohol brews: The yeast eats all the sugar and leaves your brew tasting boring and decidedly un-sweet. Adding more sugar will just kickstart the yeast again and leave you with the same problem as before, albeit with more alcohol. If you aren't planning to carbonate your beverage, you can kill the yeast with a second Campden tablet and then add sugar to taste. But if a carbonated brew is your aim, the solution is to sweeten your brew after the fact with a nonfermentable sugar.

Yeast aren't interested in nonfermentable sugars, usually because their chemical structures are too complex for yeast to digest. The most common sweeteners used in homebrewing are lactose, maltodextrin, stevia, sucralose, and aspartame. I have had the most success back-sweetening with sucralose in the form of Splenda, which sweetens with minimal aftertaste.

Add back-sweeteners to brews just before bottling. Most of them will dissolve into the brew with a little stirring, but you can also dissolve them in hot water first. Start with the ratios below, taste your brew, and then add more as desired.

» **LACTOSE:** ¾ cup / 3 ounces per gallon. Be careful of serving to people with lactose intolerance.

» **MALTODEXTRIN:** ¼ cup / 1 ounce per gallon. This powder also gives brews a more syrupy mouthfeel. Careful of using too much or you end up with Jell-O!

» **STEVIA POWDER:** ½ teaspoon per gallon.

» **SUCRALOSE (SUCH AS SPLENDA):** ¼ cup / ¼ ounce per gallon.

» **ASPARTAME (SUCH AS SWEET'N LOW OR EQUAL):** 1¼ cup / ¼ ounce per gallon.

Don't want to back-sweeten with one of these alternative sweeteners?

» Add white granulated sugar to taste and bottle as normal, but also fill one plastic soda bottle to use as an indicator for when the brew has carbonated. When the plastic bottle is rock solid with very little give, the brews are ready. Refrigerate all bottles immediately to stop carbonation and drink within a few weeks. Unrefrigerated bottles are at risk of overcarbonating and shattering.

» Add the bottling sugar to carbonate but no other additional sugar or sweeteners. When ready to serve, make a simple syrup by simmering equal parts water and sugar until the sugar has dissolved. Pour your brew into a glass and add simple syrup to taste.

Dry Apple Cider

MAKES 1 GALLON
TARGET ORIGINAL GRAVITY RANGE = 1.055–1.060
TARGET FINAL GRAVITY RANGE = 1.000–1.005
TARGET ABV = 7 PERCENT

This cider is dry in the sense that it is not very sweet tasting. All the naturally occurring sugars in the apple juice become yeast food. We're left with a hard cider that has a snappy-tart flavor, a refreshing bitterness, and an astringent edge. The balance of these flavors, as well as any lingering sweetness, depends on the apples going into your cider. If you are buying your own apples for pressing, get a mix of different apple varieties (15 pounds of apples will give you 1 gallon of juice). If buying juice, choose one with a nice complexity of flavors. If the cider ends up a bit too dry for your taste, you can sweeten it up just before bottling (see Back-Sweetening, page 71).

1 gallon apple juice, preferably unpasteurized
1 Campden tablet
1 teaspoon yeast nutrient
1 teaspoon acid blend
½ teaspoon pectic enzyme
¼ teaspoon tannin
1½ tablespoons (½ tube) liquid cider yeast
3 tablespoons / 1 ounce corn sugar dissolved in ½ cup boiling water and cooled, for bottling
1 cup / 1 ounce Splenda or other nonfermentable sugar (optional)

1 • Sanitize a 2-gallon bucket, its lid, the air lock, and a spoon for stirring.

2 • Pour the apple juice into the 2-gallon fermentation bucket. Take a hydrometer reading to determine the original gravity (see Brewer's Handbook, page 16). Crush the Campden tablet and stir it into the juice. Snap on the lid and attach the air lock. Wait 24 hours for the Campden to sterilize the juice. (If using pasteurized juice, you can skip this step.)

3 • After the juice is sterilized, prepare the yeast starter. Sanitize a measuring cup, a 1-quart canning jar, and a stirring spoon. Scoop out 1 cup of juice and pour it into the canning jar. Pour the yeast over top and cover the jar with a piece of plastic wrap secured with a rubber band. Give the jar a good shake and let it stand for 1 to 3 hours. It will become foamy, and you will see tiny bubbles popping on the surface of the liquid. Once you see some sign of activity, the starter can be used.

continued

DRY APPLE CIDER, CONTINUED

4 • Pour the starter into the juice along with the yeast nutrient, acid blend, pectic enzyme, and tannin. Stir vigorously to distribute the yeast and aerate the juice. Snap the lid back on and reattach the air lock. You should see active fermentation as evidenced by bubbles in the air lock within 48 hours.

5 • Let the cider ferment undisturbed for at least 3 days or up to 7 days, until fermentation has slowed and the sediment created during brewing has had a chance to settle. At this point, the cider is ready to be transferred off the sediment and into a smaller 1-gallon jug for the longer secondary fermentation.

6 • Sanitize a 1-gallon jug, its stopper, the racking cane, its tip, the siphon hose, and the hose clamp. Siphon all of the cider into the jug. Tilt the bucket toward the end to siphon all of the liquid. Stop when you see the liquid in the hose becoming cloudy with sediment. Seal the jug with its stopper and insert the air lock. Let it sit somewhere cool and dark for another 2 weeks.

7 • To bottle the cider, sanitize a stockpot, a hydrometer, ten 12-ounce beer bottles or six 22-ounce beer bottles, their caps, the siphon hose, the racking cane, its tip, a measuring cup, and the bottle filler. Siphon ½ cup of cider to the hydrometer and use to determine final gravity. Drink the cider or pour it back into the jug once used.

8 • Pour the corn sugar solution into the stockpot. Siphon the cider into the stockpot to mix with the corn sugar solution, splashing as little as possible. Scoop a little cider with the measuring cup and give it a taste. Add Splenda (or other back-sweetener, see page 71) if a sweeter cider is desired. Siphon the cider into bottles, cap, and label.

9 • Let the bottles sit at room temperature out of direct sunlight for at least 1 month or store for up to 1 year. Refrigerate before serving.

MAKES 1 GALLON
TARGET ORIGINAL GRAVITY RANGE = 1.095–1.100
TARGET FINAL GRAVITY RANGE = 1.005–1.000
TARGET ABV = 14 PERCENT

This cider is more properly an apple mead. Or technically, a cyser. But don't let the name throw you off because a glass of this certainly tastes like a fall cider, albeit the most heavenly, vanilla-infused, spice-bedazzled cider you've ever had the pleasure of sipping. I recommend hoarding all your bottles for cold nights spent reading by the fire in the depths of winter.

1 gallon apple juice, preferably unpasteurized
1⅓ cups / 1 pound honey
1 vanilla bean
3 cinnamon sticks
2 cloves
2 star anise
Zest from 1 orange
2 Campden tablets
1½ tablespoons (½ tube) liquid sweet mead yeast
1 teaspoon yeast nutrient
½ teaspoon pectic enzyme
1 teaspoon acid blend
⅛ teaspoon tannin

1 • Sanitize a 2-gallon bucket, its lid, the air lock, and a spoon for stirring.

2 • Pour the apple juice into the 2-gallon fermentation bucket. Warm the honey in 30-second bursts in the microwave until loose and liquidy. Stir a little juice into the honey until the honey dissolves and is pourable, and then stir all the honey into the juice. Continue stirring until the honey is completely dissolved. Split the vanilla bean down its length and scrape out the seeds. Add both the seeds and the bean to the juice, along with the cinnamon sticks, cloves, star anise, and orange zest. Take a hydrometer reading to determine the original gravity (see Brewer's Handbook, page 16).

3 • Crush 1 Campden tablet and stir it into the juice. Snap on the lid and attach the air lock. Wait 24 hours for the Campden to sterilize the juice. (If you're using pasteurized juice, you can skip this sterilizing step.)

4 • After the juice is sterilized, prepare the yeast starter. Sanitize a measuring cup, a 1-quart canning jar, and a stirring spoon. Scoop out 1 cup of juice and pour it into the jar. Pour the yeast into the jar and cover with a piece of plastic wrap secured with a rubber band. Give the jar a good shake and let it stand for 1 to 3 hours. It should become foamy, and you will see tiny bubbles popping on the surface of the liquid. Once you see some sign of activity, the starter can be used.

continued

SWEET SPICED MULLED CIDER, CONTINUED

5 • Pour the starter into the juice along with the yeast nutrient, pectic enzyme, acid blend, and tannin. Stir vigorously to distribute the yeast and aerate the juice. Snap the lid back on and reattach the air lock. You should see active fermentation as evidenced by bubbles in the air lock within 48 hours.

6 • Let the cider ferment for at least 3 days or up to 7 days, until fermentation has slowed and the sediment created during brewing has had a chance to settle. At this point, the cider is ready to be transferred off the sediment and into a smaller 1-gallon jug for the longer secondary fermentation.

7 • Sanitize a 1-gallon jug, its stopper, the racking cane, its tip, the siphon hose, and the hose clamp. Siphon all of the cider into the jug, leaving the spices behind. Tilt the bucket toward the end to siphon all of the liquid. Stop when you see the liquid in the siphon hose becoming cloudy with sediment. Seal the jug with its stopper and insert the air lock. Let it sit somewhere cool and dark for at least 2 weeks.

8 • You can continue aging the cider for up to 6 months. During this time, it's good to occasionally siphon the cider off the sediment that collects on the bottom of the jug: Siphon the cider into a sterilized stockpot, clean and sanitize the jug, and siphon the cider back into the jug. This also provides a good opportunity to taste the cider and see how it's coming along. If it tastes a little sweet, you can add extra acid blend to give it some tartness and/or some tannin to give dryness and astringency. Start with a little of these ingredients, taste after a week or two, and continue adjusting as needed. The cider can be bottled whenever it tastes good to you.

9 • When you are ready to bottle, siphon the cider into a sanitized stockpot, crush the second Campden tablet, and stir it into the cider. Clean and resanitize the jug and siphon the cider back into the jug. Wait at least 24 hours before bottling.

10 • To bottle the cider, sanitize a hydrometer, ten 12-ounce bottles or six 22-ounce bottles (or five 750-milliliter wine bottles), their caps (or corks), the siphon hose, the racking cane, its tip, and the bottle filler. Siphon ½ cup of cider to the hydrometer and use to determine final gravity. Drink the cider or pour it back into the jug once used. Siphon the cider into the bottles, cap (or cork), and label.

11 • Store the bottles in a cool, dark place for 1 month or up to 1 year. Serve at room temperature.

Pear Cider

MAKES 1 GALLON
TARGET ORIGINAL GRAVITY RANGE = 1.060–1.065
TARGET FINAL GRAVITY RANGE = 1.005–1.010
TARGET ABV = 7 PERCENT

Think of pear cider, or perry, as apple's more well-behaved, angelic younger cousin. On the whole, I find that pear cider is sweeter and less dry after fermentation than apple cider. The addition of apple juice to the brew actually helps keep it from being too sweet! If you have access to an abundance of fresh pears and a juicer, by all means make your own pear juice. It takes about 11 pounds of whole pears to make 3 quarts of juice.

12 cups pear juice, preferably unpasteurized

4 cups apple juice, preferably unpasteurized

1 Campden tablet

1 teaspoon yeast nutrient

1 teaspoon acid blend

½ teaspoon pectic enzyme

¼ teaspoon tannin

2 teaspoons (1 packet) dry white wine yeast

3 tablespoons / 1 ounce corn sugar dissolved in ½ cup boiling water and cooled, for bottling

1 cup / 1 ounce Splenda or other nonfermentable sugar (optional; see Back-Sweetening, page 71)

1 • Sanitize a 2-gallon bucket, its lid, the air lock, and a spoon for stirring.

2 • Combine the pear juice and apple juice in the 2-gallon fermentation bucket. Take a hydrometer reading to determine the original gravity (see Brewer's Handbook, page 16). Crush the Campden tablet and stir it into the juice. Snap on the lid and attach the air lock. Wait 24 hours for the Campden to sterilize the juice. (If you are using pasteurized juice, you can skip this sterilizing step.)

3 • After the juice is sterilized, prepare the yeast starter. Sanitize a measuring cup, a 1-quart canning jar, and a stirring spoon. Scoop out 1 cup of juice and pour it into the jar. Sprinkle the yeast over top and cover the jar with a piece of plastic wrap secured with a rubber band. Give the jar a good shake and let it stand for 1 to 3 hours. It should become foamy, and you will see tiny bubbles popping on the surface of the liquid. Once you see some sign of activity, the starter can be used.

4 • Pour the starter into the juice along with the yeast nutrient, acid blend, pectic enzyme, and tannin. Stir vigorously to distribute the yeast and aerate the juice. Snap the lid back on and reattach the air lock. You should see active fermentation as evidenced by bubbles in the air lock within 48 hours.

continued

PEAR CIDER, CONTINUED

5 • Let the cider ferment undisturbed for at least 3 days or up to 7 days, until fermentation has slowed and the sediment created during brewing has had a chance to settle. At this point, the cider is ready to be transferred off the sediment and into a smaller 1-gallon jug for the longer secondary fermentation.

6 • Sanitize a 1-gallon jug, its stopper, the racking cane, its tip, the siphon hose, and the hose clamp. Siphon all of the cider into the jug. Tilt the bucket toward the end to siphon all of the liquid. Stop when you see the liquid in the hose becoming cloudy with sediment. Seal the jug with its stopper and insert the air lock. Let it sit somewhere cool and dark for 2 weeks.

7 • To bottle the cider, sanitize a stockpot, a hydrometer, ten 12-ounce beer bottles or six 22-ounce beer bottles, their caps, the siphon hose, the racking cane, its tip, a measuring cup, and the bottle filler. Siphon ½ cup of cider to the hydrometer and use to determine final gravity. Drink the cider or pour it back into the jug once used.

8 • Pour the corn sugar solution into the stockpot. Siphon the cider into the stockpot to mix with the corn sugar solution, splashing as little as possible. Scoop a little cider with the measuring cup and give it a taste. Add Splenda (or other back-sweetener, see page 71) if a sweeter cider is desired. Siphon the cider into bottles, cap, and label.

9 • Let the bottles sit at room temperature out of direct sunlight for at least 1 month or store for up to 1 year. Refrigerate before serving.

Hard Lemonade

MAKES 1 GALLON
TARGET ORIGINAL GRAVITY RANGE = 1.040–1.045
TARGET FINAL GRAVITY RANGE = 1.005–1.010
TARGET ABV = 4 PERCENT

Yeast is not really a fan of acidic environ-ments. A little acidity, sure. But a lot of it? Like a big jug of lemon juice? Not so much. This is why we have to take a pro-gressive approach to making hard lem-onade at home. Coaxing the yeast along with several additions of water, sugar, and lemon juice softens the impact of the acid, and gives the yeast time to realize that lemon juice isn't so bad after all.

TOTAL INGREDIENTS

13½ cups water

1 cup / 7 ounces white granulated sugar

2 teaspoons (1 packet) dry champagne yeast

1 teaspoon yeast nutrient

3 cups freshly squeezed lemon juice (from 18 to 24 lemons)

3 tablespoons / 1 ounce corn sugar, for bottling

1 cup / 1 ounce Splenda or other nonfermentable sugar (see page 71)

DAY 1 MORNING

1 cup water

4 tablespoons white granulated sugar

2 teaspoons (1 packet) dry champagne yeast

1 • On the morning of the first day, sanitize a 2-quart canning jar and a spoon.

2 • Bring the water to a boil. Remove from the heat, stir in the sugar to dissolve, and let cool to room temperature. Pour the sugar water mixture into the canning jar, sprinkle the yeast over top, and cover the jar with a piece of plastic wrap secured with a rub-ber band. Give the jar a good shake and let it stand for 12 hours. By evening, the liquid should be very foamy and bubbly.

DAY 1 EVENING

2 cups water

2 tablespoons white granulated sugar

1 teaspoon yeast nutrient

½ cup freshly squeezed lemon juice (from 3 to 4 lemons)

continued

HARD LEMONADE, CONTINUED

3 • On the evening of the first day, bring the water to a boil. Remove from the heat and stir in the sugar and yeast nutrient to dissolve. Cool to room temperature.

4 • Pour the sugar-water mixture and lemon juice into the yeast mixture. Stir vigorously with a sanitized spoon and cover with a piece of plastic wrap secured with a rubber band.

DAY 2 MORNING

2 cups water

2 tablespoons white granulated sugar

½ cup freshly squeezed lemon juice
   (from 3 to 4 lemons)

5 • On the morning of the second day, sanitize a 1-gallon jug, stopper, an air lock, a funnel, and a measuring cup.

6 • Bring the water to a boil. Remove from the heat and stir in the sugar to dissolve. Cool to room temperature.

7 • Pour the sugar-water mixture, lemon juice, and the Day 1 mixture (sugar water, lemon juice, and the yeast starter) into the 1-gallon jug. Cover the mouth of the jug and shake vigorously. Insert the stopper and the air lock. Store the jug at room temperature away from direct sunlight.

DAY 2 EVENING

2 cups water

2 tablespoons white granulated sugar

½ cup freshly squeezed lemon juice
   (from 3 to 4 lemons)

8 • On the evening of the second day, bring the water to a boil. Remove from the heat and stir in the sugar to dissolve. Cool to room temperature.

9 • Pour this sugar water and lemon juice into the jug. Cover the mouth of the jar and shake vigorously. Insert the stopper and the air lock. Store the jug at room temperature away from direct sunlight.

DAY 3 MORNING

2 cups water

2 tablespoons white granulated sugar

½ cup freshly squeezed lemon juice
   (from 3 to 4 lemons)

10 • On the morning of the third day, bring the water to a boil. Remove from the heat and stir in the sugar to dissolve. Cool to room temperature.

11 • Pour this sugar water and lemon juice into the jug. Cover the mouth of the jar and shake vigorously. Insert the stopper and the air lock. Store the jug at room temperature away from direct sunlight.

DAY 3 EVENING

2 cups water

2 tablespoons white granulated sugar

½ cup freshly squeezed lemon juice
   (from 3 to 4 lemons)

12 • In the evening of the third day, bring the water to a boil. Remove from the heat and stir in the sugar to dissolve. Cool to room temperature.

13 • Pour this sugar water and lemon juice into the jug. Cover the mouth of the jar and shake vigorously. Insert the stopper and the air lock. Store the jug at room temperature away from direct sunlight.

DAY 4 MORNING

2 cups water

2 tablespoons white granulated sugar

½ cup freshly squeezed lemon juice
(from 3 to 4 lemons)

14 • On the morning of the fourth day, bring the water to a boil. Remove from the heat and stir in the sugar to dissolve. Cool to room temperature.

15 • Pour this sugar water and lemon juice into the jug. Cover the mouth of the jar and shake vigorously. Insert the stopper and the air lock. Store the jug at room temperature away from direct sunlight.

16 • At this point, all the ingredients for the hard lemonade have been added. Take a hydrometer reading to determine the original gravity (see Brewer's Handbook, page 16). Since fermentation has already started, this reading will be approximate. Let the lemonade continue to ferment undisturbed for another week.

DAY 11

½ cup water, for bottling

3 tablespoons / 1 ounce corn sugar, for bottling

1 cup / 1 ounce Splenda or other
nonfermentable sugar (see page 71)

17 • To bottle the lemonade, sanitize a stock-pot, a hydrometer, ten 12-ounce beer bottles or six 22-ounce beer bottles, their caps, the siphon hose, the racking cane, its tip, a measuring cup, and the bottle filler. Siphon ½ cup of lemonade into the hydrometer and use to determine final gravity. Drink the lemonade or pour it back into the jug once used.

18 • Bring the water to a boil. Add the corn sugar and Splenda and stir to dissolve. Let cool to room temperature and then pour it into the stockpot. Siphon the lemonade into the stockpot to mix with the corn sugar solution, splashing as little as possible. Scoop a little lemonade with the measuring cup and give it a taste. Add more Splenda (or other back-sweetener, see page 71) if a sweeter lemonade is desired. Siphon the lemonade into bottles, cap, and label.

19 • Let the bottles sit at room temperature out of direct sunlight for at least 1 month or store for up to 1 year. Refrigerate before serving.

Jamaican Ginger Beer

MAKES 1 GALLON
TARGET ORIGINAL GRAVITY RANGE = 1.030–1.035
TARGET FINAL GRAVITY RANGE = 1.005–1.010
TARGET ABV = 3 PERCENT

A good ginger beer should send a warning sting down the back of your throat and then kindle a gentle fire in your belly. Not from the alcohol, but from the ginger. Buy the freshest ginger you can find to ensure maximum ginger payload in your beer. The root should feel firm and heavy when you squeeze it, never pulpy or wizened. If you would like even more ginger intensity, add another few tablespoons of minced fresh ginger during the secondary fermentation.

2½ pounds gingerroot

1 gallon water

1½ cups packed / 12 ounces brown sugar

¼ cup / 1 ounce maltodextrin (optional; see page 71)

1 cup freshly squeezed lime juice (from about 8 limes)

½ teaspoon peppercorns

1 Campden tablet

1½ tablespoons (½ tube) liquid California ale yeast

1 teaspoon yeast nutrient

3 tablespoons / 1 ounce corn sugar dissolved in ½ cup boiling water and cooled, for bottling

1 cup / 1 ounce Splenda or other nonfermentable sugar (optional; see page 71)

1 • Sanitize a 2-gallon bucket, its lid, the air lock, and a spoon for stirring.

2 • Scrub the gingerroot clean. Trim away any blemishes or rough spots, but leave the skins on. Coarsely chop the ginger and combine it in the bowl of a food processor with 1 cup of the water. Blend in pulses until the gingerroot is reduced to a pulp.

3 • Bring the remaining 15 cups water to a boil. Remove the pot from heat, add the brown sugar and maltodextrin, and stir to dissolve. Stir in the lime juice, peppercorns, and gingerroot pulp. Set the pot aside until the water has completely cooled. This will take an hour or two.

4 • Pour the ginger water with ginger pulp into the 2-gallon fermentation bucket. Take a hydrometer reading to determine the original gravity (see Brewer's Handbook, page 16). Crush the Campden tablet and stir it into the water. Snap on the lid and attach the air lock. Wait 24 hours for the Campden to sterilize the brew.

5 • After the ginger water is sterilized, prepare the yeast starter. Sanitize a measuring cup, a 1-quart canning jar, and a stirring
spoon. Scoop out 1 cup of ginger water and
pour it into the canning jar. Pour the yeast
over top and cover the jar with a piece of
plastic wrap secured with a rubber band.
Give the jar a good shake and let it stand for
1 to 3 hours. It should become foamy, and
you will see tiny bubbles popping on the
surface of the liquid. Once you see some
sign of activity, the starter can be used.

6 • Pour the starter into the ginger water
along with the yeast nutrient. Stir vigorously
to distribute the yeast and aerate the water.
Snap the lid back on and reattach the air
lock. You should see active fermentation as
evidenced by bubbles in the air lock within
48 hours.

7 • Let the ginger beer ferment undisturbed
for at least 3 days or up to 7 days, until fermentation has slowed and the sediment
created during brewing has had a chance
to settle. At this point, the beer is ready to
be transferred off the sediment and into a
smaller 1-gallon jug for the longer secondary fermentation.

8 • Sanitize a 1-gallon jug, its stopper, the
racking cane, its tip, the siphon hose, and
the hose clamp. Siphon all of the ginger
beer into the jug. Tilt the bucket toward the
end to siphon all of the liquid. Stop when you
see the liquid in the siphon hose becoming
cloudy with sediment. Insert the stopper and
air lock. Let the jug sit somewhere cool and
dark for another 2 weeks.

9 • To bottle the ginger beer, sanitize a
stockpot, a hydrometer, ten 12-ounce beer
bottles or six 22-ounce beer bottles, their
caps, the siphon hose, the racking cane, its
tip, a measuring cup, and the bottle filler.
Siphon ½ cup of ginger beer to the hydrometer and use to determine final gravity.
Drink the ginger beer or pour it back into
the jug once used.

10 • Pour the corn sugar solution into the
stockpot. Siphon the ginger beer into the
stockpot to mix with the corn sugar solution,
splashing as little as possible. Scoop a little ginger beer with the measuring cup and
give it a taste. Add Splenda (or other back-
sweetener, see page 71) if a sweeter ginger
beer is desired. Siphon the ginger beer into
bottles, cap, and label.

11 • Let the bottles sit at room temperature out
of direct sunlight for at least at least 1 month
or store for up to 1 year. Refrigerate before
serving.

Pineapple–Brown Sugar Cider

MAKES 1 GALLON
TARGET ORIGINAL GRAVITY RANGE = 1.040–1.045
TARGET FINAL GRAVITY RANGE = 1.005–1.010
TARGET ABV = 4.5 PERCENT

I first heard about *tepache* from Karen Solomon's book, *Can It, Bottle It, Smoke It*, and knew immediately that I would need to make a version for myself. The traditional Mexican homebrew is made with discarded pineapple rinds and fermented in an open container with whatever wild yeasts happen to be floating by. I decided that if some is good, more is better, and threw in the whole pineapple. My control-freak tendencies also got the better of me, and I nixed the wild yeast fermentation, though you can have a go at this you're feeling adventurous. Piloncillo is an unrefined sugar used in a lot of Mexican cooking; you can usually find it sold in cones at Mexican grocery stores. If you'd like a sweeter *tepache,* add additional sweetener just before bottling (see Back-Sweetening, page 71).

1 very ripe pineapple

14 cups water

1 cup packed / 8 ounces grated piloncillo or dark brown sugar

1 cinnamon stick

2 cloves

1 Campden tablet

1½ tablespoons (½ tube) liquid Belgian ale yeast

1 teaspoon yeast nutrient

1 teaspoon acid blend

½ teaspoon pectic enzyme

1 cup / 1 ounce Splenda or other nonfermentable sugar (optional; see page 71)

3 tablespoons / 1 ounce corn sugar dissolved in ½ cup boiling water and cooled, for bottling

1 • Sanitize a 2-gallon bucket, its lid, the air lock, and a spoon for stirring.

2 • Scrub the pineapple clean. Cut away the green top and very bottom of the pineapple and discard. Cut the remaining pineapple into bite-size chunks with the peel still on.

3 • Bring the water to a boil. Remove the pot from heat, add the piloncillo, and stir to dissolve. Set the pot aside until the water has completely cooled. This will take an hour or two.

4 • Combine the brown sugar water, cinnamon, cloves, and pineapple in the 2-gallon fermentation bucket. Take a hydrometer reading to determine the original gravity (see Brewer's Handbook, page 16). Crush the Campden tablet and stir it into the water.

Snap on the lid and attach the air lock. Wait 24 hours for the Campden to sterilize the pineapple water.

5 • After the pineapple water is sterilized, prepare the yeast starter. Sanitize a measuring cup, a 1-quart canning jar, and a stirring spoon. Scoop out 1 cup of pineapple water and pour it into the jar. Pour the yeast over top and cover the jar with a piece of plastic wrap secured with a rubber band. Give the jar a good shake and let it stand for 1 to 3 hours. It should become foamy, and you will see tiny bubbles popping on the surface of the liquid. Once you see some sign of activity, the starter can be used.

6 • Pour the starter into the pineapple water along with the yeast nutrient, acid blend, and pectic enzyme. Stir vigorously to distribute the yeast and aerate the water. Snap the lid back on and reattach the air lock. You should see active fermentation as evidenced by bubbles in the air lock within 48 hours.

7 • Let the pineapple cider ferment undisturbed for at least 3 days or up to 7 days, until fermentation has slowed and the sediment created during brewing has had a chance to settle. At this point, the cider is ready to be transferred off the sediment and into a smaller 1-gallon jug for the longer secondary fermentation.

8 • Sanitize a 1-gallon jug, its stopper, the racking cane, its tip, the siphon hose, and the hose clamp. Siphon all of the cider into the jug. Tilt the bucket toward the end to siphon all of the liquid. Stop when you see the liquid in the siphon hose becoming cloudy with sediment. Insert the stopper and air lock. Let the jug sit somewhere cool and dark for 2 weeks.

9 • To bottle the cider, sanitize a stockpot, a hydrometer, ten 12-ounce beer bottles or six 22-ounce beer bottles, their caps, the siphon hose, the racking cane, its tip, a measuring cup, and the bottle filler. Siphon ½ cup of cider to the hydrometer and use to determine final gravity. Drink the cider or pour it back into the jug once used.

10 • Pour the corn sugar solution into the stockpot. Siphon the cider into the stockpot to mix with the corn sugar solution, splashing as little as possible. Scoop a little cider with the measuring cup and give it a taste. Add Splenda (or other back-sweetener, see page 71) if a sweeter cider is desired. Siphon the cider into bottles, cap, and label.

11 • Let the bottles sit at room temperature out of direct sunlight for at least 1 month or store for up to 1 year. Refrigerate before serving.

 Beer

EXPERT INTERVIEW

Dann Paquette, owner and head brewer of Pretty Things Beer and Ale Project, Somerville, Massachusetts

How did you get hooked on brewing beer?

From the moment I brewed my first batch of beer at home, I knew I wanted to be a professional brewer. Instantly. To the point that I wasn't sure if I'd ever homebrew again because I wanted to do it in a brewery. That was about 20 years ago.

What is the trickiest aspect of beer brewing to master?

Stuck mash. Boilovers. Keeping track of everything. Brewing is a one-person job for me. Any time there are any distractions, I have the potential to do something that could ruin the beer or even be physically dangerous. You have a lot of boiling wort there. I tend to not let anyone near me while I'm brewing, and I keep it very quiet. I work constantly but slowly so I can keep my brain focused on what I'm doing.

What inspires your brewing?

My early beer drinking was in the late '80s when we didn't really have a specialty beer market yet. The beers were coming over from Europe. They weren't necessarily craft brands, but they were made with all the old beer-brewing technology and using the same techniques that made them really famous 50 or 100 years earlier. Those flavors were the ones that blew my mind. I couldn't figure out how they made them. So our beers are maybe overly nostalgic. I'm trying to create flavors that are from another place.

What goes into making a new beer?

We're about 75 percent sure going into it how a beer is going to turn out. We know the raw materials, we know the aesthetic we're trying to create. Fermentation always changes things in unexpected ways, so we taste it as much as we can at every step along the way and adjust what we can.

What is one thing homebrewers could do to improve their beer?

Cleanliness is a cliché. I'm going to assume that people are going to be really clean and going to sanitize everything. The other thing would be to make sure you're pitching enough yeast and getting oxygen in the wort. Most of the problems that you taste in homebrewed beer have to do with the fermentation—they get phenolic or estery. Pitching enough yeast and whisking the wort to add oxygen will help.

PRETTY THINGS BEERS TO TRY: Jacques D'Or, St. Botolph's Town, and Baby Tree

Master Beer Recipe

MAKES 1 GALLON

Beer is malted grains steeped in water, flavored with hops, and fermented with yeast. So simple, and yet beer brewing is one of the more complex and challenging projects you will find in this book. I say this not to warn you, but to get your curious cat whiskers trembling. Here is a challenge, my friends! Brew beer, and you can brew anything.

When developing your own beer recipe, there are a few things to keep in mind. More base malts generally mean increased malty sweetness and increased alcohol. More flavoring and specialty malts will intensify the flavors of those malts in your beer. The same goes for increasing the hops. More isn't always better though, especially with hops. Too much of a high-alpha-acid hop, and your brew will be too bitter to drink (see Hops, page 93). Think about how the flavors of each ingredient will interact and use other beer recipes as a guide for making your own. If you've never brewed before, try making a few of the recipes that follow to get a feel for the ingredients and the process. Making your own beer recipe can be tricky, and you must walk before you can run, young brewing ninjas.

BREWING TERMS

BOIL: The 60-minute or longer period where the wort is boiled and hops are added in bittering, flavoring, and aroma additions.

BOTTLING SUGAR: The sugar added just before bottling in order to carbonate the beer or other homebrew. You'll sometimes hear this called "priming sugar" in the brewing world. Any sugar can be used, but corn sugar is preferred because it dissolves easily without leaving residual flavor.

HOT BREAK: When the foam collecting on the surface of the wort as it comes to a boil begins to break apart and fall back into the pot. Be careful that the wort doesn't boil over as this is happening. Stir the wort or adjust the heat as needed.

MASH: The process of steeping grains in hot water to extract their sugars. "The mash" also refers the combined grains and hot water itself.

PITCH: To add the yeast to the cooled wort.

SPARGE: To rinse the mashed grains to wash the sugars from the grains and filter the wort.

WORT: The liquid gathered after steeping grains. This is essentially unfermented beer.

YEAST STARTER

2 to 4 tablespoons dried malt extract

1 cup boiling water

1½ tablespoons (½ tube) liquid ale yeast or 2 teaspoons (1 packet) dry ale yeast

INGREDIENTS

2 gallons water

8 to 12 cups / 2 to 3 pounds base malts, milled

1 to 4 cups / 4 to 16 ounces flavoring malts, milled

1 to 2 cups / 4 to 8 ounces specialty malts, milled

1 to 2½ tablespoons / .3 to .89 ounce / 10 to 25 grams hops (bittering)

½ to 1½ tablespoons / .17 to .5 ounce / 5 to 15 grams hops (flavoring)

½ to 1½ tablespoons / .17 to .5 ounce / 5 to 15 grams hops (aroma)

⅛ teaspoon dried Irish moss (optional, for clarifying brews)

3 tablespoons / 1 ounce corn sugar dissolved in ½ cup boiling water and cooled, for bottling

FLAVORING EXTRAS

1 to 2 pounds fresh or frozen fruit

2 to 4 ounces cacao nibs or ground coffee

1 to 4 tablespoons whole herbs or spices

EQUIPMENT

1-pint canning jar

Stockpot

Measuring cups and spoons

Long-handled spoon

Instant-read thermometer

Oven thermometer (optional)

Large fine-mesh strainer

Second stockpot (optional)

1 (7-pound) bag of ice (optional)

Flour sack towel or cheesecloth

Hydrometer

2-gallon fermentation bucket with lid

Air lock

1-gallon jug

Stopper

Racking cane and tip

Siphon hose

Hose clamp

Bottle filler

Bottle caps

Bottle capper

10 (12-ounce) beer bottles or 6 (22-ounce) beer bottles

1 • Make the yeast starter 6 to 12 hours before you start to brew. Sanitize a 1-pint canning jar and a spoon. Stir 2 tablespoons of malt extract into 1 cup of boiling water until dissolved and cool to room temperature in the jar. (Use 4 tablespoons of dried malt extract if you are brewing a beer with a projected ABV of 8 percent or higher.) Add the yeast and cover the jar with a piece of plastic wrap secured with a rubber band. Give the jar a good shake and let it stand until needed. The starter should become foamy, and you will see tiny bubbles popping on the surface of the liquid. (See Brewer's Handbook, page 15.)

continued

MASTER BEER RECIPE, CONTINUED

2 • To mash the grains, warm 1 gallon of water to 160°F in a large stockpot over high heat. While doing this, preheat your oven to 150° to 155°F to create a nice, comfy environment for mashing the grains. If you don't have an oven setting this low or don't own an oven thermometer, just warm your oven for about 5 minutes on the lowest setting. Turn off your oven once it has warmed.

3 • Remove the pot of water from the heat, pour all of the grains—the base malts, flavoring malts, and specialty malts—into the water, and stir. Check the temperature of the mash. The combined water and grains should even out to about 153°F, which is the ideal temperature for sugar extraction.

4 • Cover the pot with its lid and put it in the oven. Set the timer for 1 hour. Every 15 minutes, pull the pot out, stir the grains, and check the temperature. Maintain a mash temperature of 150°F to 155°F. If it starts to drop below 150°F, set it on the burner for just a minute or two to warm it up again. If it's too warm, stir it off the heat for a few minutes to bring the temperature down.

5 • After 1 hour, your grains are mashed, meaning you have extracted all the fermentable sugars from the grains. If you had some trouble with high or low temperatures, give the mash another 15 minutes in the oven to make sure you've extracted all of the sugar.

6 • Place the pot on the stove and heat the mash to 170°F. Hold it here for about 10 minutes. This will effectively halt all the enzyme activity in the brew. While doing this, heat

3

7a
7b

8

10

BEER

liquid, now called wort, will collect in the pot beneath. Slowly pour half of the warmed water over the grains, rinsing them evenly.

8 • Clean the stockpot used for making the mash and transfer the strainer with the used grains back to this pot. Pour the wort through the grains again. This helps wash all of the sugar from the grains and strain out some of the sediment. Repeat this sparging step twice more, ending with the wort back in your original stockpot. Add enough additional warmed water to make about 1½ gallons of total wort, measuring based on the size of your pot (a 2-gallon pot will be three-quarters full). The amount of additional water needed will vary depending on the amount of grains used and how much liquid they absorbed during mashing. Discard the used grains.

9 • Bring the wort up to a rolling boil over high heat on the stove top. This will take 30 to 45 minutes. Right before the wort comes to a boil, you'll see foam collecting on the surface. Watch for this to start clumping together and falling back into the wort, called "hot break." Also be careful that the wort doesn't boil over as this is happening. Stir the wort or lower the heat as needed.

10 • Once your wort is boiling and the foam has fallen back into the wort, you're ready to start adding hops. The hop boil is typically 1 hour, and most brewing recipes will give instructions for adding hops in three additions for bittering, flavoring, and aroma.

the remaining 1 gallon of water to around 170°F in a separate pot. This will be used in the next step for sparging the grains and increasing the volume of the wort before the boiling step.

7 • To sparge the grains, set a large strainer over another large stockpot, your fermentation bucket, or another vessel large enough to hold all the liquid from the mash step, and place this in your kitchen sink. Pour the mashed grains into the strainer. The

continued

MASTER BEER RECIPE, CONTINUED

Generally, bittering hops are added at the beginning of the hop boil (with 60 minutes remaining), flavoring hops are added in the second half of the boil (with 20 minutes remaining), and aroma hops are added at the very end (with 1 minute remaining). Irish moss can be added with the flavoring hops with 20 minutes remaining in the hop boil. Other recipe add-ins like cacao nibs, fruit, or spices are usually added with the aroma hops with 1 minute left in the boil.

11 • Once the hop boil has finished, cool down the wort as quickly as you can. Ideally, you want it to reach at least 85°F within 30 minutes. This helps protein solids settle out more evenly (resulting in a smooth, clear beer) and prevents any unwanted bacteria from taking up residence. To help cool down the wort quickly, make an ice bath in your sink. Fill your sink partway with cold water and set the pot with the hot wort inside. Add ice cubes to the sink to cool the wort even more quickly. Stir the wort gently with your sanitized spoon. When the water in the sink becomes warm, change it out for cold water and more ice cubes. Repeat as necessary until the wort has cooled.

A note on the temperature: Yeast dies at 110°F. It's most comfortable at around 75°F. Cooling to 85°F is a happy compromise between keeping your yeast alive and the practicalities of cooling a large amount of liquid in a home kitchen. In reality, as long as your wort is below 100°F, the yeast will be fine.

12 • Sanitize your fermentation bucket and lid, the air lock, a long-handled spoon, a strainer, a funnel, and a hydrometer. Once your wort is cool, set the strainer over the 2-gallon fermentation bucket. If desired, line the strainer with a flour sack towel or several layers of cheesecloth (sanitized by submerging in the sanitizing solution); this will catch more sediment but also requires more time and patience. Strain the wort into the fermentation bucket. Check to make sure you have around 1 gallon of wort (the fermentation bucket should be half full). Add more water if needed; if you're a little over, don't worry about it, but make a note to add less sparge water next time. Take a hydrometer reading to determine the original gravity (see Brewer's Handbook, page 16).

12

13

HOPS

There are so many hops now available to home-brewers that you could brew with a different kind in every batch for years. The alpha acid percent (AA%) indicates the amount of bittering resin in a hop and thus its bittering potential. Hops with a high AA% are generally better used for adding bitterness to beers while hops with a lower AA% tend to be better for flavoring and adding aroma. Hops in the middle range can be used for either. Here are some of the most common in order of AA%:

SAAZ (3–5%): soft and herbal

CHALLENGER (3–6% AA): spicy and woodsy

FUGGLE (3–6% AA): earthy and spicy

HALLERTAU (4–7% AA): floral and spicy

CASCADE (4–8% AA): grapefruit and pine

PALISADE (4–8% AA): fruity and herbal

CLUSTER (5–8% AA): floral and neutrally bitter

AMARILLO (8–10% AA): citrus and floral

COLUMBUS (10–16% AA): herbal and spicy

CHINOOK (12–14%): grapefruit and pine

SORACHI ACE (13–18%): lemon candy and white pepper

If you start swapping hops, keep an eye on the alpha acid percents. Hops of similar percentages can be used one-for-one. When jumping from one level to another, use this formula:

AA% Hop A (grams Hop A) ÷ AA% Hop B = grams Hop B

Hop A is the original hop and Hop B is the substitute hop.

13 • To begin fermentation, pour the yeast starter into the wort and stir vigorously to distribute the yeast and aerate the wort. Adding oxygen back into the wort through aeration helps the yeast get going quickly during the 24 hours after brewing and ensures a strong primary fermentation. Snap on the lid and insert the air lock. Set the bucket somewhere out of the way, out of direct sunlight, and at moderate room temperature. You should see active fermentation as evidenced by bubbles in the air lock within 48 hours.

14 • Let the beer ferment undisturbed for at least 3 days or up to 7 days, until fermentation has slowed and the sediment created during brewing has had a chance to settle. At this point, the beer is ready to be transferred off the sediment and into a smaller 1-gallon jug for the longer secondary fermentation.

continued

MASTER BEER RECIPE, CONTINUED

15 • Sanitize a 1-gallon jug, its stopper, the racking cane, its tip, the siphon hose, and the hose clamp. Siphon all of the beer into the jug (see Brewer's Handbook, page 16). Tilt the bucket toward the end to siphon all of the liquid. Stop when you see the liquid in the siphon hose becoming cloudy with sediment. Seal the jug with its stopper and insert the air lock.

16 • Let the brew sit somewhere cool and dark for 2 weeks. By this point, you should see no real signs of fermentation. Watch the air lock: If 2 minutes pass without seeing any bubbles, fermentation is essentially complete. If you do see a bubble, let it sit for another several days until you no longer see any bubbles.

17 • To bottle the beer, sanitize a stockpot, a hydrometer, ten 12-ounce beer bottles or six 22-ounce beer bottles, their caps, the siphon hose, the racking cane, its tip, and the bottle filler. Siphon ½ cup of beer to the hydrometer and use to determine final gravity. Drink the beer or pour it back into the jug once used.

18 • Pour the corn sugar solution into the stockpot. Siphon the beer into the stockpot to mix with the corn sugar solution, splashing as little as possible.

19 • Siphon the beer into bottles, cap, and label. Let the bottles sit at room temperature out of direct sunlight for at least 2 weeks to fully carbonate. Store for up to 1 year. Refrigerate before serving.

17

18
19

GRAINS

Malted grains form the base of all beer recipes, and combining different kinds of grains from the categories below give us the different flavor profiles in our beers. Malting is the process of partially sprouting grains to develop their sugars, which provides food for the yeast later in the brewing process. Unmalted grains are sometimes used in brewing to add special flavors or colors, but because they are unmalted, they don't provide any additional sugar to the brew.

Base Malts

These malts have fairly neutral flavors but are high in enzymes and potential sugars. They would make yawn-inducing beers on their own but form a solid foundation for other, more flavorful malts.

AMERICAN 2-ROW: Packed with sugar, light flavor and color, and an excellent base for almost any brew.

PALE ALE: Slightly toastier in flavor and color than American 2-row with just as much fermentation potential.

MARIS OTTER: Roasting gives this malt a nuttier flavor and darker color than other base malts, but it still contains a good amount of sugar.

PILSNER: Extremely light in flavor and color, used primarily for pilsners and other lagers.

Flavoring Malts

Here is where your beer starts to pick up flavor. These malts are roasted to a greater degree, which decreases their available sugars but increases the flavor and color they can give a beer.

CRYSTAL: Actually a range of malts, all roasted different amounts. Crystal 20-degree is on the lighter end of the spectrum with sweet and breadlike flavors, while crystal 120-degree is on the other end with deeply nutty and caramelized flavors.

VIENNA: Lightly toasted. Provides a touch of malty flavor and a golden color.

MUNICH: Rich and malty. Gives beers a deep amber-red color (Caramunich has toastier and more caramelized flavors).

HONEY: Sweet and mild with a subtle clover-honey flavor.

BISCUIT: Adds a light flavor and aroma like fresh-baked bread.

Specialty Malts

A little goes a long way with these deeply roasted malts.

CHOCOLATE: Adds flavors of burnt caramel, dark fruits, cacao nibs, and yes, chocolate.

COFFEE: Like fresh-roasted coffee beans.

SPECIAL B: Adds rich flavors of raisins and toffee, along with a deep brown color.

BLACK PATENT: Very intense, bitter, roasted flavor. A small amount will color brews black.

SMOKED: Dried over wood fires, these malts add a campfire smokiness to brews.

Other Malts, Grains, and Adjuncts

Grains like these don't add much sugar for fermentation, but they contribute their own unique flavors, and occasionally textures, to the beer.

WHEAT: In small amounts, malted wheat helps give beers a foamy head. In larger quantities, it gives beers a hazy appearance, soft mouthfeel, and sweet wheaty flavor.

RYE: Adds spicy notes to beer. Careful—it can make the mash incredibly sticky.

OATS: Don't add much flavor but give beer a creamy mouthfeel.

RICE: Lightens the body of beer and adds some subtle fruity notes.

BUCKWHEAT: Gives beer a nutty, earthy flavor. Good for adding roasted depth to gluten-free beers.

Amber Ale

MAKES 1 GALLON
TARGET ORIGINAL GRAVITY RANGE = 1.060–1.065
TARGET FINAL GRAVITY RANGE = 1.015–1.020
TARGET ABV = 6 PERCENT

Malty, roasty, and just the slightest bit bitter: that's my definition of a good amber ale. It's the kind of beer that you want after an epically long day before even taking off your coat or thinking about dinner. As dependable as a favorite pair of jeans, this beer hits the spot every time.

YEAST STARTER

2 tablespoons dried malt extract

1 cup boiling water

1½ tablespoons (½ tube) liquid California ale yeast

INGREDIENTS

2 gallons water

8 cups / 2 pounds pale ale malt, milled

2 cups / 8 ounces honey malt, milled

½ cup / 2 ounces crystal 15-degree malt, milled

½ cup / 2 ounces crystal 40-degree malt, milled

½ cup / 2 ounces wheat malt, milled

1 tablespoon / .3 ounce / 10 grams Fuggle hops (bittering)

½ tablespoon / .17 ounce / 5 grams Saaz hops (flavoring)

⅛ teaspoon dried Irish moss

½ tablespoon / .17 ounce / 5 grams Saaz hops (aroma)

3 tablespoons / 1 ounce corn sugar dissolved in ½ cup boiling water and cooled, for bottling

1 • Make the yeast starter 6 to 12 hours before you plan to brew. Sanitize a 1-pint canning jar and a spoon. Stir the malt extract into the boiling water until dissolved and cool to room temperature in the jar. Add the yeast and cover the jar with a piece of plastic wrap secured with a rubber band. Give the jar a good shake and let it stand until needed. The starter should become foamy after a few hours, and you will see tiny bubbles popping on the surface of the liquid.

2 • In a large stockpot over high heat, warm 1 gallon of water to 160°F. While doing this, preheat your oven to 150°F to 155°F to create a nice, comfy environment for mashing the grains. If you don't have an oven setting this low, or don't own an oven thermometer, just warm your oven for about 5 minutes on the lowest setting. Turn off your oven once it has warmed.

3 • To make the mash, remove the pot of water from the heat, pour all the grains—the pale ale malt, honey malt, crystal 15-degree malt, crystal 40-degree malt, and wheat malt—into the water, and stir. Check the temperature of the mash with an instant-read thermometer. Stir until it reaches at least 155°F.

4 • Cover the pot and put it in the oven. Set a timer for 1 hour. Every 15 minutes, pull the pot out, stir the grains, and check the temperature. Maintain a mash temperature of 150°F to 155°F. If the temperature starts to drop below 150°F, set the pot on the burner

continued

AMBER ALE, CONTINUED

for just a minute or two to warm it up again. If it's too warm, stir the mash off the heat for a few minutes to bring the temperature down.

5 • After 1 hour, the grains are mashed. If you had trouble with high or low temperatures, give the mash another 15 minutes in the oven to make sure you've extracted all of the sugar.

6 • Place the pot on the stove and heat the mash to 170°F. Hold it at this temperature for about 10 minutes. While doing this, heat the remaining 1 gallon of water in a separate pot to around 170°F to use in the next step.

7 • To sparge the grains, set a large strainer over another large stockpot, your fermentation bucket, or another vessel large enough to hold all the liquid from the mash step, and place this in your kitchen sink. Pour the mashed grains into the strainer. The liquid, now called wort, will collect in the pot beneath. Slowly pour half of the warmed water over the grains, rinsing them evenly.

8 • Clean the stockpot used for making the mash and transfer the strainer with the used grains back to this pot. Pour the wort through the grains again. Repeat this sparging step twice more, ending with the wort back in your original stockpot. Add enough additional warmed water to make about 1½ gallons of total wort, measuring based on the size of your pot (a 2-gallon pot will be three-quarters full). The amount of additional water needed will vary depending on how much liquid the grains absorbed during mashing. Discard the used grains.

9 • Bring the wort up to a rolling boil over high heat on the stove top. This will take 30 to 45 minutes. Watch for the hot break and be careful that the wort doesn't boil over as this is happening. Stir the wort or lower the heat as needed.

10 • Set a timer for 1 hour and add 1 tablespoon Fuggle hops for bittering. With 20 minutes left, add the ½ tablespoon Saaz hops for flavoring and the Irish moss. With 1 minute left, add ½ tablespoon Saaz hops for aroma.

11 • Prepare an ice bath in your sink. Cool the wort to around 85°F, changing out the water in the ice bath as needed.

12 • Sanitize your fermentation bucket and lid, the air lock, a long-handled spoon, a strainer, a funnel, and a hydrometer. Set the strainer over the 2-gallon fermentation bucket. If desired, line the strainer with a flour sack towel or several layers of cheese-cloth (sanitized by submerging in the sanitizing solution). Strain the wort into the fermentation bucket. Check to make sure you have around 1 gallon of wort. Add more water if needed. Take a hydrometer reading to determine the original gravity (see Brewer's Handbook, page 16).

13 • Pour the yeast starter into the wort and stir vigorously to distribute the yeast and aerate the wort. Snap on the lid and insert the air lock. Set the bucket somewhere out of the way, out of direct sunlight, and at moderate room temperature. You should see active fermentation as evidenced by bubbles in the air lock within 48 hours.

14 • Let the beer ferment undisturbed for at least 3 days or up to 7 days, until fermentation has slowed and the sediment created during brewing has had a chance to settle. At this point, the beer is ready to be transferred off the sediment and into a smaller 1-gallon jug for the longer secondary fermentation.

15 • Sanitize a 1-gallon jug, its stopper, the racking cane, its tip, the siphon hose, and the hose clamp. Siphon all of the beer into the jug. Tilt the bucket toward the end to siphon all of the liquid. Stop when you see the liquid in the hose becoming cloudy with sediment. Seal the jug with its stopper. Sanitize the air lock and insert it into the jug's stopper. Let it sit somewhere cool and dark for 2 weeks.

16 • To bottle the beer, sanitize a stockpot, a hydrometer, ten 12-ounce beer bottles or six 22-ounce beer bottles, their caps, the siphon hose, the racking cane, its tip, and the bottle filler. Siphon ½ cup of beer to the hydrometer and use to determine final gravity. Drink the beer or pour it back into the jug once used.

17 • Pour the corn sugar solution into the stockpot. Siphon the beer into the stockpot to mix with the corn sugar solution, splashing as little as possible. Siphon the beer into bottles, cap, and label.

18 • Let the bottles sit at room temperature out of direct sunlight for at least 2 weeks to fully carbonate. Store for up to 1 year. Refrigerate before serving.

IPA

MAKES 1 GALLON
TARGET ORIGINAL GRAVITY RANGE = 1.060–1.065
TARGET FINAL GRAVITY RANGE = 1.015–1.020
TARGET ABV = 6 PERCENT

Cascade hops give India pale ales, aka IPAs, the tongue-twisting bitter grapefruit flavor that so many of us have come to love, but they aren't the only hops in town. Since this IPA recipe uses the same hop for bittering, flavoring, and aroma, this is a good recipe for playing around with hops. Try Citra hops for a tropical twist or East Kent Golding hops for a more British-style IPA with earthy and tealike flavors. Adjust the amounts of hops based on their alpha acid units (see page 93).

YEAST STARTER

2 tablespoons dried malt extract

1 cup boiling water

1½ tablespoons (½ tube) liquid California ale yeast

INGREDIENTS

2 gallons water

8 cups / 2 pounds American 2-row malt, milled

2 cups / 8 ounces Maris Otter malt, milled

2 cups / 8 ounces crystal 20-degree malt, milled

2½ tablespoons / .87 ounce / 25 grams Cascade hops (bittering)

1 tablespoon / .3 ounce / 10 grams Cascade hops (flavoring)

⅛ teaspoon dried Irish moss

1 tablespoon / .3 ounce / 10 grams Cascade hops (aroma)

3 tablespoons / 1 ounce corn sugar dissolved in ½ cup boiling water and cooled, for bottling

1 • Make the yeast starter 6 to 12 hours before you plan to brew. Sanitize a 1-pint canning jar and a spoon. Stir the malt extract into the boiling water until dissolved and cool to room temperature in the jar. Add the yeast and cover the jar with a piece of plastic wrap secured with a rubber band. Give the jar a good shake and let it stand until needed. The starter should become foamy after a few hours, and you will see tiny bubbles popping on the surface of the liquid.

2 • In a large stockpot over high heat, warm 1 gallon of water to 160°F. While doing this, preheat your oven to 150°F to 155°F to create a nice, comfy environment for mashing the grains. If you don't have an oven setting this low, or don't own an oven thermometer, just warm your oven for about 5 minutes on the lowest setting. Turn off your oven once it has warmed.

3 • To make the mash, remove the pot of water from the heat, pour all the grains—the American 2-row malt, Maris Otter malt, and crystal 20-degree malt—into the water, and stir. Check the temperature of the mash with an instant-read thermometer. Stir until it reaches at least 155°F.

continued

IPA, CONTINUED

4 • Cover the pot and put it in the oven. Set a timer for 1 hour. Every 15 minutes, pull the pot out, stir the grains, and check the temperature. Maintain a mash temperature of 150°F to 155°F. If the temperature starts to drop below 150°F, set the pot on the burner for just a minute or two to warm it up again. If it's too warm, stir the mash off the heat for a few minutes to bring the temperature down.

5 • After 1 hour, the grains are mashed. If you had trouble with high or low temperatures, give the mash another 15 minutes in the oven to make sure you've extracted all of the sugar.

6 • Place the pot on the stove and heat the mash to 170°F. Hold it at this temperature for about 10 minutes. While doing this, heat the remaining 1 gallon of water to around 170°F in a separate pot to use in the next step.

7 • To sparge the grains, set a large strainer over another large stockpot, your fermentation bucket, or another vessel large enough to hold all the liquid from the mash step, and place this in your kitchen sink. Pour the mashed grains into the strainer. The liquid, now called wort, will collect in the pot beneath. Slowly pour half of the warmed water over the grains, rinsing them evenly.

8 • Clean the stockpot used for making the mash and transfer the strainer with the used grains back to this pot. Pour the wort through the grains again. Repeat this sparging step twice more, ending with the wort back in your original stockpot. Add enough additional warmed water to make about 1½ gallons of total wort, measuring based on the size of your pot (a 2-gallon pot will be three-quarters full). The amount of additional water needed will vary depending on how much liquid the grains absorbed during mashing. Discard the used grains.

9 • Bring the wort up to a rolling boil over high heat on the stove top. This will take 30 to 45 minutes. Watch for the hot break and be careful that the wort doesn't boil over as this is happening. Stir the wort or lower the heat as needed.

10 • Set a timer for 1 hour and add the 2½ tablespoons Cascade hops for bittering. When 20 minutes are left, add the 1 tablespoon Cascade hops for flavoring and the Irish moss. When there is 1 minute left, add the remaining 1 tablespoon Cascade hops for aroma.

11 • Prepare an ice bath in your sink. Cool the wort to about 85°F, changing out the water in the ice bath as needed.

12 • Sanitize your fermentation bucket and lid, the air lock, a long-handled spoon, a strainer, a funnel, and a hydrometer. Set the strainer over the 2-gallon fermentation bucket. If desired, line the strainer with a flour sack towel or several layers of cheese-cloth (sanitized by submerging in the sanitizing solution). Strain the wort into the fermentation bucket. Check to make sure you have at least 1 gallon of wort. Add more water if needed. Take a hydrometer reading to determine the original gravity (see Brewer's Handbook, page 16).

13 • Pour the yeast starter into the wort and stir vigorously to distribute the yeast and aerate the wort. Snap on the lid and insert the air lock. Set the bucket somewhere out of the way, out of direct sunlight, and at moderate room temperature. You should see active fermentation as evidenced by bubbles in the air lock within 48 hours.

14 • Let the beer ferment undisturbed for at least 3 days or up to 7 days, until fermentation has slowed and the sediment created during brewing has had a chance to settle. At this point, the beer is ready to be transferred off the sediment and into a smaller 1-gallon jug for the longer secondary fermentation.

15 • Sanitize a 1-gallon jug, its stopper, the racking cane, its tip, the siphon hose, and the hose clamp. Siphon all of the beer into the jug. Tilt the bucket toward the end to siphon all of the liquid. Stop when you see the liquid in the hose becoming cloudy with sediment. Seal the jug with its stopper. Sanitize the air lock and insert it into the jug's stopper. Let it sit somewhere cool and dark for 2 weeks.

16 • To bottle the beer, sanitize a stockpot, a hydrometer, ten 12-ounce beer bottles or six 22-ounce beer bottles, their caps, the siphon hose, the racking cane, its tip, and the bottle filler. Siphon ½ cup of beer to the hydrometer and use to determine final gravity. Drink the beer or pour it back into the jug once used.

17 • Pour the corn sugar solution into the stockpot. Siphon the beer into the stockpot to mix with the corn sugar solution, splashing as little as possible. Siphon the beer into bottles, cap, and label.

18 • Let the bottles sit at room temperature out of direct sunlight for at least 2 weeks to; fully carbonate. Store for up to 1 year. Refrigerate before serving.

Apricot Wheat Ale

MAKES 1 GALLON
TARGET ORIGINAL GRAVITY RANGE = 1.060–1.065
TARGET FINAL GRAVITY RANGE = 1.015–1.020
TARGET ABV = 6 PERCENT

Wheat beers have a special affinity for fruit, in my opinion. The wheat malts give these beers a Wonder Bread sweetness and an almost creamy texture—a combination that just cries out for a cannonball of tart fruit flavor. If you can't find fresh apricots for this recipe, don't bother with dried fruits or syrups. Go with another summer fruit instead, like peaches, raspberries, or strawberries.

YEAST STARTER

2 tablespoons dried malt extract

1 cup boiling water

1½ tablespoons (½ tube) liquid
    Hefeweizen yeast

INGREDIENTS

2 gallons water

4 cups / 1 pound wheat malt, milled

4 cups / 1 pound American 2-row malt, milled

2 cups / 8 ounces crystal 15-degree malt, milled

1 tablespoon / .3 ounce / 10 grams Hallertau
    hops (bittering)

½ tablespoon / .17 ounce / 5 grams Hallertau
    hops (flavoring)

½ tablespoon / .17 ounce / 5 grams Hallertau
    hops (aroma)

1 pound fresh apricots, pitted and chopped

3 tablespoons / 1 ounce corn sugar dissolved in
    ½ cup boiling water and cooled, for bottling

1 • Make the yeast starter 6 to 12 hours before you plan to brew. Sanitize a 1-pint canning jar and a spoon. Stir the malt extract into the boiling water until dissolved and cool to room temperature in the jar. Add the yeast and cover the jar with a piece of plastic wrap secured with a rubber band. Give the jar a good shake and let it stand until needed. The starter should become foamy after a few hours, and you will see tiny bubbles popping on the surface of the liquid.

2 • In a large stockpot over high heat, warm 1 gallon of water to 160°F. While doing this, preheat your oven to 150°F to 155°F to create a nice, comfy environment for mashing the grains. If you don't have an oven setting this low, or don't own an oven thermometer, just warm your oven for about 5 minutes on the lowest setting. Turn off your oven once it has warmed.

3 • To make the mash, remove the pot of water from the heat, pour all the grains— the wheat malt, American 2-row malt, and crystal 15-degree malt—into the water, and stir. Check the temperature of the mash with an instant-read thermometer. Stir until it reaches at least 155°F.

4 • Cover the pot and put it in the oven. Set a timer for 1 hour. Every 15 minutes, pull the pot out, stir the grains, and check the temperature. Maintain a mash temperature of 150°F to 155°F. If the temperature starts to drop below 150°F, set the pot on the burner for just a minute or two to warm it up again. If it's too warm, stir the mash off the heat for a few minutes to bring the temperature down.

5 • After 1 hour, the grains are mashed. If you had trouble with high or low temperatures, give the mash another 15 minutes in the oven to make sure you've extracted all of the sugar.

6 • Place the pot on the stove and heat the mash to 170°F. Hold it at this temperature for about 10 minutes. While doing this, heat the remaining 1 gallon of water in a separate pot to around 170°F to use in the next step.

7 • To sparge the grains, set a large strainer over another large stockpot, your fermentation bucket, or another vessel large enough to hold all the liquid from the mash step, and place this in your kitchen sink. Pour the mashed grains into the strainer. The liquid, now called wort, will collect in the pot beneath. Slowly pour half of the warmed water over the grains, rinsing them evenly.

8 • Clean the stockpot used for making the mash and transfer the strainer with the used grains back to this pot. Pour the wort through the grains again. Repeat this sparging step twice more, ending with the wort back in your original stockpot. Add enough additional warmed water to make about 1½ gallons of total wort, measuring based on the size of your pot (a 2-gallon pot will be three-quarters full). The amount of additional water needed will vary depending on how much liquid the grains absorbed during mashing. Discard the used grains.

9 • Bring the wort up to a rolling boil over high heat on the stove top. This will take 30 to 45 minutes. Watch for the hot break and be careful that the wort doesn't boil over as this is happening. Stir the wort or lower the heat as needed.

10 • Set a timer for 60 minutes and add the 1 tablespoon Hallertau hops for bittering. When 20 minutes are left, add the ½ tablespoon Hallertau hops for flavoring. When 1 minute is left, add the ½ tablespoon Hallertau hops for aroma and the chopped apricots. Make sure the wort comes back to a boil before removing it from the heat.

11 • Prepare an ice bath in your sink. Cool the wort to around 85°F, changing out the water in the ice bath as needed.

12 • Sanitize your fermentation bucket and lid, the air lock, a long-handled spoon, and a hydrometer. Pour the wort and apricot pieces into the sanitized 2-gallon bucket. Take a hydrometer reading to determine the original gravity (see Brewer's Handbook, page 16).

13 • Pour the yeast starter into the wort and stir vigorously to distribute the yeast and aerate the wort. Snap on the lid and insert the air lock. Set the bucket somewhere out of the way, out of direct sunlight, and at moderate room temperature. You should see active fermentation as evidenced by bubbles in the air lock within 48 hours.

continued

APRICOT WHEAT ALE, CONTINUED

14 • Let the beer ferment undisturbed for at least 3 days or up to 7 days, until fermentation has slowed and the sediment created during brewing has had a chance to settle. At this point, the beer is ready to be transferred off the sediment and apricots, and into a smaller 1-gallon jug for the longer secondary fermentation.

15 • Sanitize a 1-gallon jug, its stopper, a funnel, a flour sack towel or cheesecloth, and long-handled spoon. Insert the funnel into the 1-gallon jug and line it with the cloth. Slowly pour the beer into the jug, filtering out the solids. Use the spoon as necessary to stir up the sediment collecting in the funnel. Seal the jug with its stopper. Sanitize the air lock and insert it into the jug's stopper. Let it sit somewhere cool and dark for 2 weeks.

16 • To bottle the beer, sanitize a stockpot, a hydrometer, ten 12-ounce beer bottles or six 22-ounce beer bottles, their caps, the siphon hose, the racking cane, its tip, and the bottle filler. Siphon ½ cup of beer to the hydrometer and use to determine final gravity. Drink the beer or pour it back into the jug once used.

17 • Pour the corn sugar solution into the stockpot. Siphon the beer into the stockpot to mix with the corn sugar solution, splashing as little as possible. Siphon the beer into bottles, cap, and label.

18 • Let the bottles sit at room temperature, out of direct sunlight for at least 2 weeks to fully carbonate. Store for up to 1 year. Refrigerate before serving.

Saison Farmhouse Ale

MAKES 1 GALLON
TARGET ORIGINAL GRAVITY RANGE = 1.060–1.065
TARGET FINAL GRAVITY RANGE = 1.025–1.030
TARGET ABV = 4.5 PERCENT

Like the seasonal farmhands who originally swigged this style of beer on their lunch breaks, farmhouse ales are a bit rough around the edges. Hazy in appearance, prickly on the tongue, and packed with juicy citrus flavors, the intention here is to refresh and revive. Note that this beer has a slightly longer boil time than the others; this reduces grainy flavors.

YEAST STARTER

2 tablespoons dried malt extract

1 cup boiling water

1½ tablespoons (½ tube) liquid Saison yeast

INGREDIENTS

10 cups / 2½ pounds pilsner malt, milled

1 cup / 4 ounces wheat malt, milled

1 cup / 4 ounces Munich malt, milled

1 tablespoon / .3 ounce / 10 grams Palisade hops (bittering)

½ teaspoon / .05 ounce / 1.5 grams Sorachi Ace hops (flavoring)

½ teaspoon / .05 ounce / 1.5 grams Sorachi Ace hops (aroma)

3 tablespoons / 1 ounce corn sugar dissolved in ½ cup boiling water and cooled, for bottling

1 • Make the yeast starter 6 to 12 hours before you plan to brew. Sanitize a 1-pint canning jar and a spoon. Stir the malt extract into the boiling water until dissolved and cool to room temperature in the jar. Add the yeast and cover the jar with a piece of plastic wrap secured with a rubber band. Give the jar a good shake and let it stand until needed. The starter should become foamy after a few hours, and you will see tiny bubbles popping on the surface of the liquid.

2 • In a large stockpot over high heat, warm 1 gallon of water to 160°F. While doing this, preheat your oven to 150°F to 155°F to create a nice, comfy environment for mashing the grains. If you don't have an oven setting this low, or don't own an oven thermometer, just warm your oven for about 5 minutes on the lowest setting. Turn off your oven once it has warmed.

3 • To make the mash, remove the pot of water from the heat, pour all the grains— the pilsner malt, wheat malt, and Munich malt—into the water, and stir. Check the temperature of the mash with an instant-read thermometer. Stir until it reaches at least 155°F.

4 • Cover the pot and put it in the oven. Set a timer for 1 hour. Every 15 minutes, pull the pot out, stir the grains, and check the temperature. Maintain a mash temperature of 150°F to 155°F. If the temperature starts to drop below 150°F, set the pot on the burner

continued

SAISON FARMHOUSE ALE, CONTINUED

for just a minute or two to warm it up again. If it's too warm, stir the mash off the heat for a few minutes to bring the temperature down.

5 • After 1 hour, the grains are mashed. If you had trouble with high or low temperatures, give the mash another 15 minutes in the oven to make sure you've extracted all of the sugar.

6 • Place the pot on the stove and heat the mash to 170°F. Hold the mash at this temperature for about 10 minutes. While doing this, heat the remaining 1 gallon of water in a separate pot to around 170°F to use for the next step.

7 • To sparge the grains, set a large strainer over another large stockpot, your fermentation bucket, or another vessel large enough to hold all the liquid from the mash step, and place this in your kitchen sink. Pour the mashed grains into the strainer. The liquid, now called wort, will collect in the pot beneath. Slowly pour half of the warmed water over the grains, rinsing them evenly.

8 • Clean the stockpot used for making the mash and transfer the strainer with the used grains back to this pot. Pour the wort through the grains again. Repeat this sparging step twice more, ending with the wort back in your original stockpot. Add enough additional warmed water to make about 1¾ gallons of total wort, measuring based on the size of your pot (a 2-gallon pot will be nearly full). The amount of additional water needed

will vary depending on how much liquid the grains absorbed during mashing. Discard the used grains.

9 • Bring the wort up to a rolling boil over high heat on the stove top. This will take 30 to 45 minutes. Watch for the hot break and be careful that the wort doesn't boil over as this is happening. Stir the wort or lower the heat as needed.

10 • Set a timer for 90 minutes. Let the wort boil for 30 minutes, and then add the 1 tablespoon Palisade hops for bittering. When 20 minutes are left, add the ½ teaspoon Sorachi Ace hops for flavoring. When 1 minute is left, add the ½ teaspoon Sorachi Ace hops for aroma.

11 • Prepare an ice bath in your sink. Cool the wort to around 85°F, changing out the water in the ice bath as needed.

12 • Sanitize your fermentation bucket and lid, the air lock, a long-handled spoon, a strainer, a funnel, and a hydrometer. Set the strainer over the 2-gallon fermentation bucket. If desired, line the strainer with a flour sack towel or several layers of cheesecloth (sanitized by submerging in the sanitizing solution). Strain the wort into the fermentation bucket. Check to make sure you have at least 1 gallon of wort. Add more water if needed. Take a hydrometer reading to determine the original gravity (see Brewer's Handbook, page 16).

13 • Pour the yeast starter into the wort and stir vigorously to distribute the yeast and aerate the wort. Snap on the lid and insert the air lock. Set the bucket somewhere out of the way, out of direct sunlight, and at moderate room temperature. You should see active fermentation as evidenced by bubbles in the air lock within 48 hours.

14 • Let the beer ferment undisturbed for at least 3 days or up to 7 days, until fermentation has slowed and the sediment created during brewing has had a chance to settle. At this point, the beer is ready to be transferred off the sediment and into a smaller 1-gallon jug for the longer secondary fermentation.

15 • Sanitize a 1-gallon jug, its stopper, the racking cane, its tip, the siphon hose, and the hose clamp. Siphon all of the beer into the jug. Tilt the bucket toward the end to siphon all of the liquid. Stop when you see the liquid in the hose becoming cloudy with sediment. Seal the jug with its stopper. Sanitize the air lock and insert it into the jug's stopper. Let it sit somewhere cool and dark for 2 weeks.

16 • To bottle the beer, sanitize a stockpot, a hydrometer, ten 12-ounce beer bottles or six 22-ounce beer bottles, their caps, the siphon hose, the racking cane, its tip, and the bottle filler. Siphon ½ cup of beer to the hydrometer and use to determine final gravity. Drink the beer or pour it back into the jug once used.

17 • Pour the corn sugar solution into the stockpot. Siphon the beer into the stockpot to mix with the corn sugar solution, splashing as little as possible. Siphon the beer into bottles, cap, and label.

18 • Let the bottles sit at room temperature out of direct sunlight for at least 2 weeks to fully carbonate. Store for up to 1 year. Refrigerate before serving.

Gluten-Free Pale Ale

MAKES 1 GALLON
TARGET ORIGINAL GRAVITY RANGE = 1.045–1.050
TARGET FINAL GRAVITY RANGE = 1.010–1.015
TARGET ABV = 5 PERCENT

Going gluten free means giving up many beloved foods. Beer should not be one of them. Sorghum is the closest gluten-free equivalent to a base malt, though it's currently only commercially available as a syrup. It tastes like a cross between brown sugar and honey, and it plays nicely with the whole range of hops. Other grains, such as buckwheat and quinoa, give gluten-free beers more depth and character. Be sure to use dry yeasts when brewing gluten-free beers since liquid yeasts are cultured with barley malts.

YEAST STARTER

2 tablespoons sorghum extract

1 cup boiling water

2 teaspoons (1 packet) dry ale yeast (such as Safale US-05)

INGREDIENTS

1½ gallons water

1¼ cups / 8 ounces toasted buckwheat groats

2⅛ cups / 1½ pounds sorghum extract

2 tablespoons / .7 ounce / 20 grams Cluster hops (bittering)

1 tablespoon / .3 ounce / 10 grams Cluster hops (flavoring)

⅛ teaspoon dried Irish moss

1 tablespoon / .3 ounce / 10 grams Saaz hops (aroma)

3 tablespoons / 1 ounce corn sugar dissolved in ½ cup boiling water and cooled, for bottling

1 • Make the yeast starter 1 to 3 hours before you plan to brew. Sanitize a 1-pint canning jar and a spoon. Stir 2 tablespoons of sorghum extract into 1 cup of boiling water until dissolved and cool to room temperature in the jar. Add the yeast and cover the jar with a piece of plastic wrap secured with a rubber band. Give the jar a good shake and let it stand until needed. The starter should become foamy after a few hours, and you will see tiny bubbles popping on the surface of the liquid.

2 • In a large stockpot over high heat, warm 8 cups of water to 155°F. While doing this, preheat your oven to 150°F to 155°F to create a nice, comfy environment for mashing the grains. If you don't have an oven setting this low, or don't own an oven thermometer, just warm your oven for about 5 minutes on the lowest setting. Turn off your oven once it has warmed.

continued

GLUTEN-FREE PALE ALE, CONTINUED

3 • Remove the pot of water from the heat, pour the buckwheat into the water, and stir. Check the temperature of the mash with an instant-read thermometer. Stir until it reaches at least 155°F.

4 • Cover the pot and put it in the oven. Set a timer for 30 minutes. Halfway through, pull the pot out, stir the grains, and check the temperature. Maintain a mash temperature of 150°F to 155°F. If the temperature starts to drop below 150°F, set the pot on the burner for just a minute or two to warm it up again. If it's too warm, stir the mash off the heat for a few minutes to bring the temperature down.

5 • After 30 minutes, the buckwheat is mashed. Place the pot on the stove and heat the mash to 170°F. Hold it at this temperature for about 10 minutes. While doing this, heat the remaining 1 gallon of water to around 170°F in a separate pot to use for the next step.

6 • To sparge the grains, set a large strainer over another large stockpot, your fermentation bucket, or another vessel large enough to hold all the liquid from the mash step, and place this in your kitchen sink. Pour the mashed grains into the strainer. The liquid, now called wort, will collect in the pot beneath. Slowly pour half of the warmed water over the grains, rinsing them evenly.

7 • Clean the stockpot used for making the mash and transfer the strainer with the used grains back to this pot. Pour the wort through the grains again. Repeat this sparging step twice more, ending with the wort back in your original stockpot.

8 • Add 1½ pounds sorghum extract and enough additional warmed water to make about 1½ gallons of total wort, measuring based on the size of your pot (a 2-gallon pot will be three-quarters full). The amount of additional water needed will vary depending on how much liquid the grains absorbed during mashing. Discard the used grains.

9 • Bring the wort up to a rolling boil over high heat on the stove top. This will take 30 to 45 minutes. Watch for the hot break and be careful that the wort doesn't boil over as this is happening. Stir the wort or lower the heat as needed.

10 • Set a timer for 60 minutes and add the 2 tablespoons Cluster hops for bittering. When 20 minutes are left, add the 1 tablespoon Cluster hops for flavoring and the Irish moss. When 1 minute is left, add the 1 tablespoon Saaz hops for aroma.

11 • Prepare an ice bath in your sink. Cool the wort to around 85°F, changing out the water in the sink as needed.

12 • Sanitize your fermentation bucket and lid, the air lock, a long-handled spoon, a strainer, a funnel, and a hydrometer. Set the strainer over the 2-gallon fermentation bucket. If desired, line the strainer with a flour sack towel or several layers of cheese-cloth (sanitized by submerging in the sanitizing solution). Strain the wort into the fermentation bucket. Check to make sure you have at least 1 gallon of wort. Add more water if needed. Take a hydrometer reading to determine the original gravity (see Brewer's Handbook, page 16).

13 • Pour the yeast starter into the wort and stir vigorously to distribute the yeast and aerate the wort. Snap on the lid and insert the air lock. Set the bucket somewhere out of the way, out of direct sunlight, and at moderate room temperature. You should see active fermentation as evidenced by bubbles in the air lock within 48 hours.

14 • Let the beer ferment undisturbed for at least 3 days or up to 7 days, until fermentation has slowed and the sediment created during brewing has had a chance to settle. At this point, the beer is ready to be transferred off the sediment and into a smaller 1-gallon jug for the longer secondary fermentation.

15 • Sanitize a 1-gallon jug, its stopper, the racking cane, its tip, the siphon hose, and the hose clamp. Siphon all of the beer into the jug. Tilt the bucket toward the end to siphon all of the liquid. Stop when you see the liquid in the hose becoming cloudy with sediment. Seal the jug with its stopper. Sanitize the air lock and insert it into the jug's stopper. Let it sit somewhere cool and dark for 2 weeks.

16 • To bottle the beer, sanitize a stockpot, a hydrometer, ten 12-ounce beer bottles or six 22-ounce beer bottles, their caps, the siphon hose, the racking cane, its tip, and the bottle filler. Siphon ½ cup of beer to the hydrometer and use to determine final gravity. Drink the beer or pour it back into the jug once used.

17 • Pour the corn sugar solution into the stockpot. Siphon the beer into the stockpot to mix with the corn sugar solution, splashing as little as possible. Siphon the beer into bottles, cap, and label.

18 • Let the bottles sit at room temperature out of direct sunlight for at least 2 weeks to fully carbonate. Store for up to 1 year. Refrigerate before serving.

Mocha Stout

MAKES 1 GALLON
TARGET ORIGINAL GRAVITY RANGE = 1.055–1.060
TARGET FINAL GRAVITY RANGE = 1.020–1.035
TARGET ABV = 5 PERCENT

It doesn't take much to tip a dark and roasty flavored stout into mocha territory. The malts themselves already give the beer plenty of tantalizing coffee bean and dark chocolate flavors, especially with a handful of barley so thoroughly roasted it looks black. My secret ingredient to a truly mocha-y mocha stout is cacao nibs. They impart a rich chocolate flavor without making the beer taste too bitter or too sweet. The Goldilocks of brews, this one is just right. Note that this beer uses slightly less bottling sugar than other recipes to give it a smoother mouthfeel.

YEAST STARTER

2 tablespoons dried malt extract

1 cup boiling water

1½ tablespoons (½ tube) liquid London ale yeast

INGREDIENTS

2 gallons water

8 cups / 2 pounds Maris Otter malt, milled

1 cup / 4 ounces roasted barley, milled

1 cup / 4 ounces Caramunich malt, milled

1 cup / 4 ounces rolled oats

1½ tablespoons / .5 ounce / 15 grams Fuggle hops (bittering)

½ tablespoon / .17 ounce / 5 grams Palisade hops (aroma)

½ cup / 2 ounces cacao nibs, coarsely ground

2½ tablespoons / .75 ounce corn sugar dissolved in ½ cup boiling water, for bottling

1 • Make the yeast starter 6 to 12 hours before you start to brew. Sanitize a 1-pint canning jar and a spoon. Stir the malt extract into the boiling water until dissolved and cool to room temperature in the jar. Add the yeast and cover the jar with a piece of plastic wrap secured with a rubber band. Give the jar a good shake and let it stand until needed. The starter should become foamy after a few hours, and you will see tiny bubbles popping on the surface of the liquid.

2 • In a large stockpot over high heat, warm 1 gallon of water to 160°F. While doing this, preheat your oven to 150°F to 155°F to create a nice, comfy environment for mashing the grains. If you don't have an oven setting this low, or don't own an oven thermometer, just warm your oven for about 5 minutes on the lowest setting. Turn off your oven once it has warmed.

continued

MOCHA STOUT, CONTINUED

3 • Remove the pot of water from the heat, pour all the grains—the Maris Otter malts, roasted barley, Caramunich malts, and flaked oats—into the water, and stir. Check the temperature of the mash with an instant-read thermometer. Stir until it reaches at least 155°F.

4 • Cover the pot and put it in the oven. Set a timer for 1 hour. Every 15 minutes, pull the pot out, stir the grains, and check the temperature. Maintain a mash temperature of 150°F to 155°F. If the temperature starts to drop below 150°F, set the pot on the burner for just a minute or two to warm it up again. If it's too warm, stir the mash off the heat for a few minutes to bring the temperature down.

5 • After 1 hour, the grains are mashed. If you had trouble with high or low temperatures, give the mash another 15 minutes in the oven to make sure you've extracted all of the sugar.

6 • Place the pot on the stove and heat the mash to 170°F. Hold it at this temperature for about 10 minutes. While doing this, heat the remaining 1 gallon of water to around 170°F in a separate pot to use in the next step.

7 • To sparge the grains, set a large strainer over another large stockpot, your fermentation bucket, or another vessel large enough to hold all the liquid from the mash step, and place this in your kitchen sink. Pour the mashed grains into the strainer. The liquid, now called wort, will collect in the pot beneath. Slowly pour half of the warmed water over the grains, rinsing them evenly.

8 • Clean the stockpot used for making the mash and transfer the strainer with the used grains back to this pot. Pour the wort through the grains again. Repeat this sparging step twice more, ending with the wort back in your original stockpot. Add enough additional warmed water to make about 1½ gallons of total wort, measuring based on the size of your pot (a 2-gallon pot will be three-quarters full). The amount of additional water needed will vary depending on how much liquid the grains absorbed during mashing. Discard the used grains.

9 • Bring the wort up to a rolling boil over high heat on the stove top. This will take 30 to 45 minutes. Watch for the hot break and be careful that the wort doesn't boil over as this is happening. Stir the wort or lower the heat as needed.

10 • Set a timer for 60 minutes and add the Fuggle hops for bittering. When 1 minute is left, add the Palisade hops for aroma and the cacao nibs.

11 • Prepare an ice bath in your sink. Cool the wort to around 85°F, changing out the water in the ice bath as needed.

12 • Sanitize your fermentation bucket and lid, the air lock, a long-handled spoon, a strainer, a funnel, and a hydrometer. Set the strainer over the 2-gallon fermentation bucket. If desired, line the strainer with a flour sack towel or several layers of cheesecloth (sanitized by submerging in the sanitizing solution). Strain the wort into the fermentation bucket. Check to make sure you have around 1 gallon of wort. Add more water if needed. Take a hydrometer reading to determine the original gravity (see Brewer's Handbook, page 16).

13 • Pour the yeast starter into the wort and stir vigorously to distribute the yeast and aerate the wort. Snap on the lid and insert the air lock. Set the bucket somewhere out of the way, out of direct sunlight, and at moderate room temperature.

14 • You should see active fermentation as evidenced by bubbles in the air lock within 48 hours. Let the beer ferment undisturbed for at least 3 days or up to 7 days, until fermentation has slowed and the sediment created during brewing has had a chance to settle. At this point, the beer is ready to be transferred off the sediment and into a smaller 1-gallon jug for the longer secondary fermentation.

15 • Sanitize a 1-gallon jug, its stopper, the racking cane, its tip, the siphon hose, and the hose clamp. Siphon all of the beer into the jug. Tilt the bucket toward the end to siphon all of the liquid. Stop when you see the liquid in the hose becoming cloudy with sediment. Seal the jug with its stopper. Sanitize the air lock and insert it into the jug's stopper. Let it sit somewhere cool and dark for another 2 weeks.

16 • To bottle the beer, sanitize a stockpot, a hydrometer, ten 12-ounce beer bottles or six 22-ounce beer bottles, their caps, the siphon hose, the racking cane, its tip, and the bottle filler. Siphon ½ cup of beer to the hydrometer and use to determine final gravity. Drink the beer or pour it back into the jug once used.

17 • Pour the corn sugar solution into the stockpot. Siphon the beer into the stockpot to mix with the corn sugar solution, splashing as little as possible. Siphon the beer into bottles, cap, and label.

18 • Let the bottles sit at room temperature out of direct sunlight for at least 2 weeks to fully carbonate. Store for up to 1 year. Refrigerate before serving.

CHAPTER 6

Mead

EXPERT INTERVIEW

Oron Benary, owner and head mead-maker at Brothers Drake Meadery, Columbus, Ohio

How did you get hooked on brewing mead?

I hadn't really brewed mead at all before jumping into it with Brothers Drake. I was friends with one of the original brothers, and when he had this idea of making meads commercially, he brought me in as an investor. The way I got actively involved was because the company was about to go out of business. I decided to move to Columbus, take over the inventory, and build up the company. I learned mead-making really fast.

What is your mead-making philosophy?

The most important thing for us is using the highest-quality ingredients, period. The higher the quality of honey you use, the higher the quality of mead you get. At Brothers Drake, we're using as local honey as we can find. These are real Ohio bees. They make different honey than bees or honeys that are imported. Our meads are like fine wines.

What is the trickiest aspect of mead-making to master?

Stuck fermentation. Honey doesn't have any nutrition in it for the yeast. What is the yeast going to eat? We add yeast nutrients to help it get going, and you have to add nutrients at the right time so fermentation doesn't happen too quickly and change the flavor of the mead. Feed the yeast when it's hungry. Feed it and have it come back for more.

What is inspiring you right now?

Unfiltered mead is really exciting. It's cloudy and has more stuff in there to taste, which changes the whole flavor profile. We're also getting into using different local products. For example, pawpaws! We have a pawpaw mead now that's unbelievable.

What is one thing homebrewers could do to improve their meads?

Sanitation and keeping it away from oxygen. Keep everything sanitized and clean. Period. Get into the habit of "wash, rinse, sanitize." It's labor intensive, but even the smallest amount of bacteria can ruin the delicate nature of fermented honey. And then use the best ingredients. Spend the extra bucks to get the best ingredients you can find.

BROTHERS DRAKE MEADS TO TRY: Wild Ohio, Apple Pie, and Bergamot Blue

MAKES 1 GALLON

Mead is honey wine, pure and simple. It has a reputation for being syrupy-sweet and potent enough to knock you on your backside, but this doesn't need to be the case. Meads can be as delicate and tart as a Sauvignon Blanc or as rich and complex as a dessert wine. They will always retain the essential flavor of the honey with which they were brewed. One thing is true: Meads take time. Most meads only begin to mellow and show their true character about 6 months after brewing, though a year is even better. This isn't to say you can't drink them earlier, but try to squirrel away at least a bottle or two for deferred enjoyment.

Your aim is to make a gallon of mead, so base your initial measurements of water, honey, and fruit (if using) on making a gallon of liquid. If you do choose to use fruit, don't forget to allow for the juiciness of the fruit and the fact that you will strain out the solids after the primary fermentation. This all takes a little guesswork, and it's fine if you come in a little over or under a gallon. When deciding how much honey or fruit to use based on the recipe below, remember that more honey will make a sweeter mead and more fruit will give the mead a more prominent fruit flavor.

INGREDIENTS

12 to 14 cups water

2⅔ to 5⅓ cups / 2 to 4 pounds honey

1 to 4 pounds fruit (optional)

2 Campden tablets

1 teaspoon yeast nutrient

1 teaspoon acid blend

½ teaspoon pectic enzyme (if using fruit)

⅛ teaspoon tannin

YEAST STARTER

1 cup boiling water

2 to 4 tablespoons honey

2 teaspoons (1 package) dry champagne yeast (for dry mead) or 1½ tablespoons (½ tube) sweet mead yeast (for sweet mead)

⅛ teaspoon yeast nutrient

EQUIPMENT

Stockpot

Measuring cups and spoons

Long-handled spoon

2-gallon fermentation bucket with lid

Air lock

Mesh bag (for fruit, if using)

Hydrometer

1-pint canning jar

1-gallon jug

Stopper

Racking cane and tip

Siphon hose

Hose clamp

Bottle filler

Bottle caps or wine corks

10 (12-ounce) bottles, 6 (22-ounce) bottles, or 5 (750-milliliter) wine bottles

Bottle caps or wine corks

Bottle capper or wine corker

1 • Sanitize the 2-gallon bucket, its lid, the air lock, and a spoon for stirring.

2 • Bring the water to a simmer over medium-high heat and stir in the honey. Stir just until the honey dissolves, then remove the pot from the heat. Let stand until cooled to room temperature.

3 • Pour the honey water into the 2-gallon bucket. Coarsely chop any fruit being used into bite-size pieces (berries and small fruits can be kept whole) and secure them in a mesh bag before adding them to the honey water. Take a hydrometer reading to determine the original gravity (see Brewer's Handbook, page 16). Crush 1 Campden tablet and stir it in. Snap on the lid and attach the air lock. Wait 24 hours for the Campden to sterilize the mead.

4 • Prepare the yeast starter 12 hours after adding the Campden. Sanitize a 1-pint canning jar and a spoon. Measure out 1 tablespoon of honey for every pound going into the recipe. Stir this honey into 1 cup of boiling water until dissolved, and cool to room temperature in the jar. Add the yeast and ⅛ teaspoon of the yeast nutrient, and cover the jar with a piece of plastic wrap secured with a rubber band. Give the jar a good shake and let it stand until needed. The starter should become foamy, and you will see tiny bubbles popping on the surface of the liquid.

5 • After the honey water is sterilized, pour in the yeast starter along with the remaining 1 teaspoon yeast nutrient, acid blend, pectic

HOW TO AMP UP THE FRUIT FLAVOR

If you'd like to add a fruity power boost to your mead (or cider, beer, or wine), try adding an additional ½ to 1 pound of fruit during the secondary fermentation. The bulk of the fermenting is done at this point, so the flavors and aromas of the fruit juice stay pure and intact. The alcohol content of the brew will also protect against infection from any unwelcome bacteria or wild yeast introduced by the raw fruit.

enzyme (if using fruit), and tannin. Stir vigorously to distribute the yeast and aerate the honey water. Snap the lid back on and reattach the air lock. You should see active fermentation as evidenced by bubbles in the air lock within 48 hours.

6 • Let the mead ferment for 1 week, stirring daily with a sanitized spoon. After this time, the mead is ready to be transferred into a 1-gallon jug for the secondary fermentation.

7 • Sanitize a 1-gallon jug, stopper, the racking cane, its tip, the siphon hose, and the hose clamp. Remove the mesh bag of fruits, spices, or herbs with clean hands, and then siphon all of the mead into the jug. Tilt the bucket toward the end to siphon all of the liquid. Stop when you see the liquid in the hose becoming cloudy with sediment. If you used a very pulpy fruit, straining the mead through a sanitized flour sack towel or several layers of cheesecloth during this step can help eliminate excess sediment (see Vanilla-Peach Mead, page 130).

continued

MASTER MEAD RECIPE, CONTINUED

8 • Seal the jug with its stopper. Sanitize the air lock and insert it into the jug's stopper. Let it sit somewhere cool and dark for 4 weeks.

9 • By this point, you should see no real signs of fermentation. Watch the air lock: if 2 minutes pass without seeing any bubbles, fermentation is essentially complete. You can bottle the mead now, or continue aging it for up to 6 months.

10 • If you are continuing to age, it's good to occasionally rack (siphon) the mead off the sediment that collects on the bottom of the jug. Sanitize a stockpot, the siphon hose, the racking cane, and its tip. Siphon the mead into the stockpot. Clean and sanitize the jug, stopper, and air lock, and siphon the mead back into the jug. Insert the stopper and air lock. This also provides a good opportunity to taste the mead and see how it's coming along. If it tastes a little sweet, you can add extra acid blend to give it some tartness or some tannin to give dryness and astringency. Start with a little of these ingredients,

taste after a week or two, and continue adjusting as needed. The mead can be bottled whenever it tastes good to you.

11 • When ready to bottle, sanitize a stockpot, the siphon hose, the racking cane, and its tip. Siphon the mead into the stockpot, crush the remaining Campden tablet, and stir it into the mead. Clean and sanitize the jug, stopper, and air lock, and siphon the mead back into the jug. Insert the stopper and air lock. Wait at least 24 hours before bottling.

12 • To bottle the mead, sanitize ten 12-ounce bottles or six 22-ounce bottles (or five 750-milliliter wine bottles), their caps (or corks), the siphon hose, the racking cane, its tip, the bottle filler, and a hydrometer. Siphon ½ cup of mead to the hydrometer and use to determine final gravity. Drink the mead or pour it back into the jug once used. Siphon the mead into the bottles, cap (or cork), and label.

13 • Store the bottles in a cool, dark place for at least 2 weeks or up to 1 year.

Dry Mead

MAKES 1 GALLON
TARGET ORIGINAL GRAVITY RANGE = 1.100–1.105
TARGET FINAL GRAVITY RANGE = 1.010–1.015
TARGET ABV = 12.5 PERCENT

I confess: I am not really a fan of overly sweet beverages. I might have quietly scratched meads off my Brewing Bucket List if a friend hadn't recommended I try making a dry mead: one with less honey than the average sweet mead, leaving very little unfermented honey in the finished mead. Imagine my surprise when I poured myself a glass a few months after brewing and found that this mead…wasn't sweet. Oh, it definitely tasted like honey. But it was also dry and crisp and held haunting flavors of tropical fruits. This was the mead for me.

INGREDIENTS

12 cups water
3⅓ cups / 2½ pounds honey
2 Campden tablets
1 teaspoon yeast nutrient
1 teaspoon acid blend
⅛ teaspoon tannin

YEAST STARTER

2½ tablespoons honey
1 cup boiling water
2 teaspoons (1 packet) dry champagne yeast
⅛ teaspoon yeast nutrient

1 • Sanitize a 2-gallon bucket, its lid, the air lock, and a spoon for stirring.

2 • Bring the water to a simmer over medium-high heat and stir in the honey. Stir just until the honey dissolves and then remove from heat. Let stand until cooled to room temperature.

3 • Pour the honey water into the 2-gallon bucket. Take a hydrometer reading to determine the original gravity (see Brewer's Handbook, page 16). Crush 1 Campden tablet and stir it in. Snap on the lid and attach the air lock. Wait 24 hours for the Campden to sterilize the mead.

4 • Prepare the yeast starter 12 hours after adding the Campden. Sanitize a 1-pint canning jar and a spoon. Stir 2½ tablespoons of honey into 1 cup of boiling water until dissolved, and cool to room temperature in the jar. Add the yeast and ⅛ teaspoon yeast nutrient, and cover the jar with a piece of plastic wrap secured with a rubber band. Give the jar a good shake and let it stand until needed. The starter should become foamy, and you will see tiny bubbles popping on the surface of the liquid.

5 • After the honey water is sterilized, pour in the yeast starter along with the 1 teaspoon yeast nutrient, acid blend, and tannin. Stir vigorously to distribute the yeast and aerate the honey water. Snap the lid back on and reattach the air lock. You should see active fermentation as evidenced by bubbles in the air lock within 48 hours.

continued

DRY MEAD, CONTINUED

6 • Let the mead ferment for 1 week, stirring daily with a sanitized spoon. Then transfer the mead into a 1-gallon jug for the secondary fermentation.

7 • Sanitize a 1-gallon jug, its stopper, the racking cane, its tip, the siphon hose, and the hose clamp. Siphon all of the mead into the jug. Tilt the bucket toward the end to siphon all of the liquid. Stop when you see the liquid in the hose becoming cloudy with sediment.

8 • Seal the jug with its stopper. Sanitize the air lock and insert it into the jug's stopper. Let it sit somewhere cool and dark for 4 weeks. Bottle the mead or continue aging it for up to 6 months.

9 • If you are continuing to age, it's good to occasionally rack the mead off the sediment that collects on the bottom of the jug. Sanitize a stockpot, the siphon hose, the racking cane, and its tip. Siphon the mead into the stockpot. Clean and sanitize the jug, stopper, and air lock, and siphon the mead back into the jug. Insert the stopper and air lock. You can sample the mead and adjust the acid or tannins to your taste during this step.

10 • When ready to bottle, sanitize a stockpot, the siphon hose, the racking cane, and its tip. Siphon the mead into the stockpot, crush the remaining Campden tablet, and stir it into the mead. Clean and sanitize the jug, stopper, and air lock, and siphon the mead back into the jug. Insert the stopper and air lock. Wait at least 24 hours before bottling.

11 • To bottle the mead, sanitize ten 12-ounce bottles or six 22-ounce bottles (or five 750-milliliter wine bottles), their caps (or corks), the siphon hose, the racking cane, its tip, the bottle filler, and a hydrometer. Siphon ½ cup of mead to the hydrometer and use to determine final gravity. Drink the mead or pour it back into the jug once used. Siphon the mead into the bottles, cap (or cork), and label.

12 • Store the bottles in a cool, dark place for 2 weeks or up to 1 year. Serve chilled or at room temperature.

Chai-Spiced Mead

MAKES 1 GALLON
TARGET ORIGINAL GRAVITY RANGE = 1.130–1.135
TARGET FINAL GRAVITY RANGE = 1.025–1.030
TARGET ABV = 16 PERCENT

Spiced meads get a fancy name. They're called metheglins. When I think of honey and spices together in the same glass, I inevitably start craving a warm cup of chai. The spicy flavors of cinnamon, cardamom, and clove in traditional chai tea translate beautifully into mead form. A cup of this mead might not warm your fingers like a cup of chai, but it will still make you feel toasty.

INGREDIENTS

14 cups water

4 cups / 3 pounds honey

10 bags black tea, or 2½ tablespoons loose black tea

8 cardamom pods

½ teaspoon peppercorns

2 cloves

2 cinnamon sticks

1 vanilla bean

3-inch piece fresh gingerroot, peeled and minced

2 Campden tablets

1 teaspoon yeast nutrient

1 teaspoon acid blend

YEAST STARTER

3 tablespoons honey

1 cup boiling water

1½ tablespoons (½ tube) liquid sweet mead yeast

⅛ teaspoon yeast nutrient

1 • Sanitize a 2-gallon bucket, its lid, the air lock, and a spoon for stirring.

2 • Bring the water to a simmer over medium-high heat and stir in the honey. Stir just until the honey dissolves and then remove from heat. Add the tea and let stand until cooled to room temperature.

3 • Preheat the oven to 350°F. Combine the cardamom, peppercorns, cloves, and cinnamon in a metal pie pan and toast for 5 minutes. When cool enough to handle, put all the spices in a ziplock plastic bag and crush with a rolling pin. Split the vanilla bean down its length and scrape out the seeds. Add the spices, the vanilla beans and seed pod, and the minced ginger to the 2-gallon bucket.

4 • Remove the used tea bags (or strain out the loose tea) and pour the cooled honey water into the bucket with the spices. Take a hydrometer reading to determine the original gravity (see Brewer's Handbook, page 16). Crush 1 Campden tablet and stir it in. Snap on the lid and attach the air lock. Wait 24 hours for the Campden to sterilize the mead.

5 • Prepare the yeast starter 12 hours after adding the Campden. Sanitize a 1-pint canning jar and a spoon. Stir 3 tablespoons of

continued

CHAI-SPICED MEAD, CONTINUED

honey into 1 cup of boiling water until dissolved, and cool to room temperature in the jar. Add the yeast and ⅛ teaspoon yeast nutrient, and cover the jar with a piece of plastic wrap secured with a rubber band. Give the jar a good shake and let it stand until needed. The starter should become foamy, and you will see tiny bubbles popping on the surface of the liquid.

6 • After the honey water is sterilized, pour in the yeast starter along with the 1 teaspoon yeast nutrient and acid blend. Stir vigorously to distribute the yeast and aerate the honey water. Snap the lid back on and reattach the air lock. You should see active fermentation as evidenced by bubbles in the air lock within 48 hours.

7 • Let the mead ferment for 1 week, stirring daily with a sanitized spoon. Then transfer the mead into a 1-gallon jug for the secondary fermentation.

8 • Sanitize a 1-gallon jug, its stopper, the racking cane, its tip, the siphon hose, and the hose clamp. Siphon all of the mead into the jug, leaving the spices in the bucket. Tilt the bucket toward the end to siphon all of the liquid. Stop when you see the liquid in the hose becoming cloudy with sediment.

9 • Seal the jug with its stopper. Sanitize the air lock and insert it into the jug's stopper. Let it sit somewhere cool and dark for 4 weeks. Bottle the mead or continue aging it for up to 6 months.

10 • If you are continuing to age, it's good to occasionally rack the mead off the sediment that collects on the bottom of the jug. Sanitize a stockpot, the siphon hose, the racking cane, and its tip. Siphon the mead into the stockpot. Clean and sanitize the jug, stopper, and air lock, and siphon the mead back into the jug. Insert the stopper and air lock. You can sample the mead and adjust the acid or tannins to your taste during this step.

11 • When ready to bottle, sanitize a stockpot, the siphon hose, the racking cane, and its tip. Siphon the mead into the stockpot, crush the second Campden tablet, and stir it into the mead. Clean and sanitize the jug, stopper, and air lock, and siphon the mead back into the jug. Insert the stopper and air lock. Wait at least 24 hours before bottling.

12 • To bottle the mead, sanitize ten 12-ounce bottles or six 22-ounce bottles (or five 750-milliliter wine bottles), their caps (or corks), the siphon hose, the racking cane, its tip, the bottle filler, and a hydrometer. Siphon ½ cup of mead to the hydrometer and use to determine final gravity. Drink the mead or pour it back into the jug once used. Siphon the mead into the bottles, cap (or cork), and label.

13 • Store the bottles in a cool, dark place for 2 weeks or up to 1 year. Serve at room temperature.

Renaissance Fair Sweet Mead

MAKES 1 GALLON
TARGET ORIGINAL GRAVITY RANGE = 1.140–1.145
TARGET FINAL GRAVITY RANGE = 1.020–1.025
TARGET ABV = 19 PERCENT

If you're headed to a Renaissance fair, this is the mead you want in your flask. It is shockingly sweet and sure to have you roaring ballads in no time. If the fair isn't your destination, I will just say that this mead makes a superb dinner party finale. Pour small tumblers for your guests after the plates are cleared and don't even bother serving another dessert.

INGREDIENTS

12 cups water
4¾ cups / 3½ pounds honey
2 Campden tablets
1 teaspoon yeast nutrient
1 teaspoon acid blend
⅛ teaspoon tannin

YEAST STARTER

3½ tablespoons honey
1 cup boiling water
3 tablespoons (1 tube) liquid sweet mead yeast
⅛ teaspoon yeast nutrient

1 • Sanitize a 2-gallon bucket, its lid, the air lock, and a spoon for stirring.

2 • Bring the water to a simmer and stir in the honey. Stir just until the honey dissolves and then remove from heat. Let stand until cooled to room temperature.

3 • Pour the honey water into the 2-gallon bucket. Take a hydrometer reading to determine the original gravity (see Brewer's Handbook, page 16). Crush 1 Campden tablet and stir it in. Snap on the lid and attach the air lock. Wait 24 hours for the Campden to sterilize the mead.

4 • Prepare the yeast starter 12 hours after adding the Campden. Sanitize a 1-pint canning jar and a spoon. Stir 3½ tablespoons of honey into 1 cup of boiling water until dissolved, and cool to room temperature in the jar. Add the yeast and ⅛ teaspoon yeast nutrient, and cover the jar with a piece of plastic wrap secured with a rubber band. Give the jar a good shake and let it stand until needed. The starter should become foamy, and you will see tiny bubbles popping on the surface of the liquid.

5 • After the honey water is sterilized, pour in the yeast starter along with the 1 teaspoon yeast nutrient, acid blend, and tannin. Stir vigorously to distribute the yeast and aerate the honey water. Snap the lid back on and reattach the air lock. You should see active fermentation as evidenced by bubbles in the air lock within 48 hours.

6 • Let the mead ferment for 1 week, stirring daily with a sanitized spoon. Then transfer the mead into a 1-gallon jug for the secondary fermentation.

7 • Sanitize a 1-gallon jug, its stopper, the racking cane, its tip, the siphon hose, and the hose clamp. Siphon all of the mead into the jug. Tilt the bucket toward the end to siphon all of the liquid. Stop when you see the liquid in the hose becoming cloudy with sediment.

8 • Seal the jug with its stopper. Sanitize the air lock and insert it into the jug's stopper. Let it sit somewhere cool and dark for 4 weeks. Bottle the mead or continue aging it for up to 6 months.

9 • If you are continuing to age, it's good to occasionally rack the mead off the sediment that collects on the bottom of the jug. Sanitize a stockpot, the siphon hose, the racking cane, and its tip. Siphon the mead into the stockpot. Clean and sanitize the jug, stopper, and air lock, and siphon the mead back into the jug. Insert the stopper and air lock. You can sample the mead and adjust the acid or tannins to your taste during this step.

10 • When ready to bottle, sanitize a stockpot, the siphon hose, the racking cane, and its tip. Siphon the mead into the stockpot, crush the remaining Campden tablet, and stir it into the mead. Clean and sanitize the jug, stopper, and air lock, and siphon the mead back into the jug. Insert the stopper and air lock. Wait at least 24 hours before bottling.

11 • To bottle the mead, sanitize ten 12-ounce bottles or six 22-ounce bottles (or five 750-milliliter wine bottles), their caps (or corks), the siphon hose, the racking cane, its tip, the bottle filler, and a hydrometer. Siphon ½ cup of mead to the hydrometer and use to determine final gravity. Drink the mead or pour it back into the jug once used. Siphon the mead into the bottles, cap (or cork), and label.

12 • Store the bottles in a cool, dark place for 2 weeks or up to 1 year. Serve at room temperature.

Vanilla-Peach Mead

MAKES 1 GALLON
TARGET ORIGINAL GRAVITY RANGE = 1.085–1.090
TARGET FINAL GRAVITY RANGE = 1.000–1.005
TARGET ABV = 12 PERCENT

Mead brewed with fruit is properly called a melomel, which is awfully fun to say three times fast. This one tastes like sun-ripened peaches drizzled with honey and baked with a vanilla bean tucked into the dish. I kid you not. Definitely give this mead a full 8 months to a year to mellow out before drinking; before then, it's a bit too reminiscent of the fuzzy peach skin.

INGREDIENTS

4 pounds peaches
1 vanilla bean
14 cups water
3⅓ cups / 2½ pounds honey
2 Campden tablets
1 teaspoon acid blend
1 teaspoon yeast nutrient
½ teaspoon pectic enzyme
⅛ teaspoon tannin

YEAST STARTER

2½ tablespoons honey
1 cup boiling water
2 teaspoons (1 packet) dry champagne yeast
⅛ teaspoon yeast nutrient

1 • Sanitize a 2-gallon bucket, its lid, the air lock, and a spoon for stirring.

2 • Bring a small pot of water to a boil over high heat. Working in batches, add the peaches and blanch for about 1 minute. Remove with a slotted spoon and set aside on a clean plate. Let the water return to a boil before blanching the next batch. When cool enough to handle, pull off the peach skins with a paring knife. Coarsely chop the peaches, discarding the skins and pits. Split the vanilla bean down its length and scrape out the seeds. Add the seeds directly to the 2-gallon bucket. Put the vanilla bean pod along with the chopped peaches in a mesh bag and place in the 2-gallon bucket.

3 • Bring the water for the mead to a simmer over medium-high heat and stir in the honey. Stir just until the honey dissolves and then remove from heat. Let stand until cooled to room temperature.

4 • Pour the cooled honey water into the 2-gallon bucket with the peaches. Using a potato masher or very clean hands, mash the submerged bag of fruit to extract as much juice as possible. Take a hydrometer reading to determine the original gravity (see Brewer's Handbook, page 16). Crush 1 Campden tablet and stir it in. Snap on the lid and attach the air lock. Wait 24 hours for the Campden to sterilize the mead.

5 • Prepare the yeast starter 12 hours after adding the Campden. Sanitize a 1-pint canning jar and a spoon. Stir 2½ tablespoons of honey into 1 cup of boiling water until

dissolved, and cool to room temperature in the jar. Add the yeast and ⅛ teaspoon yeast nutrient, and cover the jar with a piece of plastic wrap secured with a rubber band. Give the jar a good shake and let it stand until needed. The starter should become foamy, and you will see tiny bubbles popping on the surface of the liquid.

6 • After the honey water is sterilized, pour in the yeast starter along with the acid blend, 1 teaspoon yeast nutrient, pectic enzyme, and tannin. Stir vigorously to distribute the yeast and aerate the honey water. Snap the lid back on and reattach the air lock. You should see active fermentation as evidenced by bubbles in the air lock within 48 hours.

7 • Let the mead ferment for 1 week, stirring daily with a sanitized spoon. Then transfer into a 1-gallon jug for the secondary fermentation.

8 • Sanitize a 1-gallon jug, its stopper, a strainer, a funnel, a flour sack towel or cheesecloth, and a long-handled spoon. Pull out the bag of peaches with clean hands and squeeze gently to extract as much liquid as possible. Insert the funnel into the 1-gallon jug and line it with the cloth. Slowly pour the mead into the jug, filtering out the solids. Use the spoon as necessary to stir up the sediment that collects in the funnel. Seal the jug with its stopper and insert the air lock.

9 • Let the mead sit somewhere cool and dark for 4 weeks. Then bottle the mead or continue aging it for up to 6 months.

10 • If you are continuing to age, it's good to occasionally rack the mead off the sediment that collects on the bottom of the jug. Sanitize a stockpot, the siphon hose, the racking cane, and its tip. Siphon the mead into the stockpot. Clean and sanitize the jug, stopper, and air lock, and siphon the mead back into the jug. Insert the stopper and air lock. You can sample the mead and adjust the acid or tannins to your taste during this step.

11 • When ready to bottle, sanitize a stockpot, the siphon hose, the racking cane, and its tip. Siphon the mead into the stockpot, crush the remaining Campden tablet, and stir it into the mead. Clean and sanitize the jug, stopper, and air lock, and siphon the mead back into the jug. Insert the stopper and air lock. Wait at least 24 hours before bottling.

12 • To bottle the mead, sanitize ten 12-ounce bottles or six 22-ounce bottles (or five 750-milliliter wine bottles), their caps (or corks), the siphon hose, the racking cane, its tip, the bottle filler, and a hydrometer. Siphon ½ cup of mead to the hydrometer and use to determine final gravity. Drink the mead or pour it back into the jug once used. Siphon the mead into the bottles, cap (or cork), and label.

13 • Store the bottles in a cool, dark place for 8 months or up to 1 year. Serve chilled or at room temperature.

Cranberry Mead

MAKES 1 GALLON
TARGET ORIGINAL GRAVITY RANGE = 1.100–1.105
TARGET FINAL GRAVITY RANGE = 1.000–1.005
TARGET ABV = 14 PERCENT

Here's what you do: The day after Thanksgiving, skip the mall and buy up all the bags of cranberries you can find. Make a few batches of cranberry mead and sock them away in the back of a closet. Forget about them for about 12 months. Remember them just in time to open a few bottles for Thanksgiving dinner. Drink, enjoy, repeat. You're welcome.

INGREDIENTS

14 cups water
4 cups / 3 pounds honey
1½ pounds cranberries
2 Campden tablets
1 teaspoon acid blend
1 teaspoon yeast nutrient
½ teaspoon pectic enzyme

YEAST STARTER

3 tablespoons honey
1 cup boiling water
1½ tablespoons (½ tube) liquid sweet
    mead yeast
⅛ teaspoon yeast nutrient

1 • Sanitize a 2-gallon bucket, its lid, the air lock, and a spoon for stirring.

2 • Bring the water to a simmer over medium-high heat and stir in the honey. Stir just until the honey dissolves and then remove from heat. Let stand until cooled to room temperature.

3 • Pour the cooled honey water into the 2-gallon bucket. Coarsely chop the cranberries, secure them in a mesh bag, and add to the honey water. Using a potato masher or very clean hands, mash the submerged bag of fruit to extract as much juice as possible. Take a hydrometer reading to determine the original gravity (see Brewer's Handbook, page 16). Crush 1 Campden tablet and stir it in. Snap on the lid and attach the air lock. Wait 24 hours for the Campden to sterilize the mead.

4 • Prepare the yeast starter 12 hours after adding the Campden. Sanitize a 1-pint canning jar and a spoon. Stir 3 tablespoons of honey into 1 cup of boiling water until dissolved, and cool to room temperature in the jar. Add the yeast and ⅛ teaspoon yeast nutrient, and cover the jar with a piece of plastic wrap secured with a rubber band. Give the jar a good shake and let it stand until needed. The starter should become foamy, and you will see tiny bubbles popping on the surface of the liquid.

5 • After the honey water is sterilized, pour in the yeast starter along with the acid blend, 1 teaspoon yeast nutrient, and pectic enzyme. Stir vigorously to distribute the yeast and aerate the honey water. Snap the lid back on and reattach the air lock. You should see active fermentation as evidenced by bubbles in the air lock within 48 hours.

6 • Let the mead ferment for 1 week, stirring daily with a sanitized spoon. Then the mead is ready to transfer into a 1-gallon jug for the secondary fermentation.

7 • Sanitize a 1-gallon jug, its stopper, the racking cane, its tip, the siphon hose, and the hose clamp. Remove the bag and discard the cranberries, then siphon all of the mead into the jug. Tilt the bucket toward the end to siphon all of the liquid. Stop when you see the liquid in the hose becoming cloudy with sediment.

8 • Seal the jug with its stopper. Sanitize the air lock and insert it into the jug's stopper. Let it sit somewhere cool and dark for 4 weeks. Bottle the mead or continue aging it for up to 6 months.

9 • If you are continuing to age, it's good to occasionally rack the mead off the sediment that collects on the bottom of the jug. Sanitize a stockpot, the siphon hose, the racking cane, and its tip. Siphon the mead into the stockpot. Clean and sanitize the jug, stopper, and air lock, and siphon the mead back into the jug. Insert the stopper and air lock. You can sample the mead and adjust the acid or tannins to your taste during this step.

10 • When ready to bottle, sanitize a stockpot, the siphon hose, the racking cane, and its tip. Siphon the mead into the stockpot, crush the remaining Campden tablet, and

stir it into the mead. Clean and sanitize the jug, stopper, and air lock, and siphon the mead back into the jug. Insert the stopper and air lock. Wait at least 24 hours before bottling.

11 • To bottle the mead, sanitize ten 12-ounce bottles or six 22-ounce bottles (or five 750-milliliter wine bottles), their caps (or corks), the siphon hose, the racking cane, its tip, the bottle filler, and a hydrometer. Siphon ½ cup of mead to the hydrometer and use to determine final gravity. Drink the mead or pour it back into the jug once used. Siphon the mead into the bottles, cap (or cork), and label.

12 • Store the bottles in a cool, dark place for 2 weeks or up to 1 year. Serve at room temperature.

Blueberry-Lavender Mead

MAKES 1 GALLON
TARGET ORIGINAL GRAVITY RANGE = 1.105–1.110
TARGET FINAL GRAVITY RANGE = 1.005–1.010
TARGET ABV = 15 PERCENT

You can ask for no better nightcap than a glass of this fine mead. Lavender is a well-known soother of worries and bringer of sweet dreams. Pairing it with mild and delicate blueberries only increases its soporific superpowers.

INGREDIENTS

14 cups water

3⅓ cups / 2½ pounds honey

1 pound blueberries

2 tablespoons dried lavender, or 3 tablespoons fresh lavender blossoms

2 Campden tablets

1 teaspoon yeast nutrient

2 teaspoons acid blend

½ teaspoon pectic enzyme

⅛ teaspoon tannin

YEAST STARTER

2½ tablespoons honey

1 cup boiling water

1½ tablespoons (½ tube) liquid sweet mead yeast

⅛ teaspoon yeast nutrient

1 • Sanitize a 2-gallon bucket, its lid, the air lock, and a spoon for stirring.

2 • Bring the water to a simmer and stir in the honey. Stir just until the honey dissolves and then remove from heat. Let stand until cooled to room temperature.

3 • Pour the honey water into the 2-gallon bucket. Secure the blueberries and lavender in a mesh bag and add them to the honey water. Using a potato masher or very clean hands, mash the submerged bag of fruit to extract as much juice as possible. Take a hydrometer reading to determine the original gravity (see Brewer's Handbook, page 16). Crush 1 Campden tablet and stir it in. Snap on the lid and attach the air lock. Wait 24 hours for the Campden to sterilize the mead.

4 • Prepare the yeast starter 12 hours after adding the Campden. Sanitize a 1-pint canning jar and a spoon. Stir 2½ tablespoons of honey into 1 cup of boiling water until dissolved, and cool to room temperature in the jar. Add the yeast and ⅛ teaspoon yeast nutrient, and cover the jar with a piece of plastic wrap secured with a rubber band. Give the jar a good shake and let it stand until needed. The starter should become foamy, and you will see tiny bubbles popping on the surface of the liquid.

5 • After the honey water is sterilized, pour in the yeast starter along with the 1 teaspoon yeast nutrient, acid blend, pectic enzyme, and tannin. Stir vigorously to distribute the yeast and aerate the honey water. Snap the lid back on and reattach the air lock. You should see active fermentation as evidenced by bubbles in the air lock within 48 hours.

6 • Let the mead ferment for 1 week, stirring daily with a sanitized spoon. Then transfer the mead into a 1-gallon jug for the secondary fermentation.

7 • Sanitize a 1-gallon jug, its stopper, the racking cane, its tip, the siphon hose, and the hose clamp. Remove the bag and discard the blueberries and lavender, and then siphon all of the mead into the jug. Tilt the bucket toward the end to siphon all of the liquid. Stop when you see the liquid in the hose becoming cloudy with sediment.

8 • Seal the jug with its stopper. Sanitize the air lock and insert it into the jug's stopper. Let it sit somewhere cool and dark for 4 weeks. Bottle the mead or continue aging it for up to 6 months.

9 • If you are continuing to age, it's good to occasionally rack the mead off the sediment that collects on the bottom of the jug. Sanitize a stockpot, the siphon hose, the racking cane, and its tip. Siphon the mead into the stockpot. Clean and sanitize the jug, stopper, and air lock, and siphon the mead back into the jug. Insert the stopper and air lock. You can sample the mead and adjust the acid or tannins to your taste during this step.

10 • When ready to bottle, sanitize a stockpot, the siphon hose, the racking cane, and its tip. Siphon the mead into the stockpot, crush the remaining Campden tablet, and stir it into the mead. Clean and sanitize the jug, stopper, and air lock, and siphon the mead back into the jug. Insert the stopper and air lock. Wait at least 24 hours before bottling.

11 • To bottle the mead, sanitize ten 12-ounce bottles or six 22-ounce bottles (or five 750-milliliter wine bottles), their caps (or corks), the siphon hose, the racking cane, its tip, the bottle filler, and a hydrometer. Siphon ½ cup of mead to the hydrometer and use to determine final gravity. Drink the mead or pour it back into the jug once used. Siphon the mead into the bottles, cap (or cork), and label.

12 • Store the bottles in a cool, dark place for 2 weeks or up to 1 year. Serve at room temperature.

Sake

Greg Lorenz, head brewer at SakéOne, Forest Grove, Oregon

How did you get hooked on brewing sake?

I'm actually a lab tech with a degree in plant biology. Since there aren't too many sake brewers in the U.S., I had a lucky chance to interview for this position at SakéOne. The culturing here is very similar to culturing in a lab and from my point of view, this is just a really big lab.

What is the trickiest aspect of sake-making to master?

Brewing is tricky because you can't actually see the yeast or the koji spore, you can only see their result. I can't look at the individual fibers of koji, but I can see the heat it produces and draw conclusions about what's going on with the koji. It's difficult to look at these secondary characteristics and draw conclusions about the primary thing.

What inspires your brewing?

For me, brewing sake is an interaction with nature. I get to look at two different natural organisms and watch them over time. I live with them, I see how they respond, I see a new nuance that doesn't seem significant but then produces a really nice flavor profile. So watching these living organisms really closely and seeing how they express flavor based on their environment is really fascinating to me.

How can you change the flavor of the sake?

Every aspect can be manipulated to give you different effects. If you think of sake as being from rice, koji, yeast, and water, then you have four different ingredients. A change to any of these will affect the flavor of the sake. Just figure out which changes matter over time.

What is one thing homebrewers could do to improve their sake?

Control the environment as much as possible. If we mess around with the temperature by a few degrees, that's a big difference. Buy a cheap fridge and use it to control the temperature and make adjustments. Any kind of rigged-up thing where you get to control the temperature of the brewing vessel is helpful. You'll probably need to put in a little more of a maverick effort into brewing sake. If you go into this expecting a weekend project, you might be a little disappointed. But if you're totally curious, and this catches your interest, then you'll be fine.

SAKÉONE SAKES TO TRY: Pearl (nigori-style sake) and G (cask-strength sake)

Master Sake Recipe #1 (Easy)

MAKES 1 GALLON

Sake is made from rice. Steamed rice, to be exact. Two different things are required to transform that steamed rice into alcohol: koji rice and yeast. Koji rice has been inoculated with a special mold spore, and enzymes produced by that mold are what ultimately break down the rice starches into fermentable sugars. Those sugars, in turn, become food for the yeast. It's called parallel fermentation, but I prefer to call it friendship. Homebrewed sake has a stronger, fruitier, and sometimes harsher taste than commercial sake, which is made in much more controlled circumstances and is also usually filtered significantly before bottling. Homebrewed sake is different, but still amazing stuff. I recommend serving all homebrewed sake chilled.

INGREDIENTS

10 cups / 5 pounds sake rice, short-grained rice, or sushi-grade medium-grain rice

2½ cups / 1¼ pounds koji rice (page 146, or see Resources, page 176)

1 gallon dechlorinated water (see page 14)

½ teaspoon acid blend

1 teaspoon yeast nutrient

1½ tablespoons (½ tube) liquid sake or lager yeast, or 2 teaspoons (1 packet) dry white wine yeast

EQUIPMENT

2-gallon fermentation bucket with lid

Air lock

Measuring cups and spoons

Long-handled spoon

Large fine-mesh strainer

Flour sack towel

Stockpot

1-gallon jug

Stopper

Funnel

Racking cane and tip

Siphon hose

Hose clamp

Bottle filler

10 (12-ounce) bottles, 6 (22-ounce) bottles, or 5 (750-milliliter) wine bottles

Bottle caps or wine corks

Bottle capper or wine corker

1 • Sanitize the 2-gallon bucket, its lid, a long-handled spoon, and the air lock.

2 • Soak, steam, and cool the rice as described on page 140.

3 • Combine the steamed rice, koji rice, water, acid blend, yeast nutrient, and yeast in the fermentation bucket. If you are steaming your rice in batches, combine everything in the fermenter with the first batch and add the remaining rice as it is cooled and ready.

4 • Snap on the lid and attach the air lock. Store the sake somewhere cool and dark, ideally around 55°F. Higher fermentation temperatures are okay but will yield stronger-tasting sake. You should see active fermentation as evidenced by bubbles in the air lock within 48 hours.

5 • Ferment the sake for 2 weeks, stirring daily with a sanitized spoon. By the end of this time, the sake usually has a good balance of sweet and sour flavors. You can stop fermentation now or continue fermenting for another week or two. The sake will gradually become less sweet and more sour.

6 • To finish and bottle the sake, sanitize a strainer, flour sack towel, stockpot, funnel, a 1-gallon jug, and its stopper.

7 • First, pour the sake through the strainer into the stockpot. Discard all the rice solids. Set the funnel in the 1-gallon jug and line it with the flour sack towel. Strain the sake again, this time into the jug. Because of all of the rice sediment, this can take a few hours. Stir the liquid in the funnel frequently to prevent the sediment from compacting and slowing down straining. If the flour sack towel becomes clogged, rinse it out, sanitize it, and replace.

8 • Clean the stockpot. Set the jug of sake, uncovered, inside the pot and fill the pot with water until the water is level with the surface of the sake. Set the pot over medium heat. Warm the sake to 140°F to pasteurize

the sake and stop the koji and yeast activity (this does not affect the alcohol content). Allow the sake to cool.

9 • For nigori-style "cloudy" sake, sanitize ten 12-ounce bottles or six 22-ounce bottles (or five 750-milliliter wine bottles), their caps (or corks), the siphon hose, the racking cane, its tip, and the bottle filler. Shake the jug of sake to make sure the sediment is fully suspended in the sake during bottling. Siphon the sake into the bottles, shaking the jug again if the sediment begins to settle. Cap (or cork) the bottles and label. Sake can be drunk immediately or aged for up to 1 year. Shake the bottle before serving and serve chilled.

10 • For clear sake, sanitize the stopper and air lock. Insert the stopper and air lock into the jug containing the pasteurized and cooled sake, and store the sake somewhere cool and dark for several days, during which time any remaining rice sediment will settle to the bottom of the jug.

11 • To bottle, sanitize ten 12-ounce bottles or six 22-ounce bottles (or five 750-milliliter wine bottles), their caps (or corks), the siphon hose, the racking cane, its tip, and the bottle filler. Siphon the sake into sanitized bottles, holding the tip of the racking cane just above the surface of the sediment. Cap (or cork) the bottles and label.

12 • Store the bottles in a cool, dark place for 2 weeks or up to 1 year. Serve chilled.

HOW TO PREPARE RICE FOR SAKE

Use this method for preparing rice in all of the sake recipes.

Rinse the rice several times in cool water to remove as much of the starch as possible. The rinsing water will be very cloudy at first and then clear over several rinses. It's okay if the water is still slightly hazy.

Cover the rice with more cool water and let it soak: 1 hour for sake-milled rice and 2 hours for short-grain or medium-grain table rice. Pour the rice into a strainer and let it drain for 1 hour.

Bring an inch or two of water to a simmer in a stockpot over low heat. Line a large strainer with a flour sack towel, letting the excess hang over the sides. Transfer the rice to the cloth-lined strainer and fold the ends of the towel over the rice to form a neat package. Set the strainer

with the rice over the stockpot and cover with a lid. If your strainer isn't big enough to hold all of the rice, work in batches. (Alternatively, you can steam rice in a bamboo steamer. Do not use a rice cooker.)

Steam the rice, covered, for 40 to 50 minutes. Stir it every 15 minutes, making sure to scrape the rice from the bottom and thoroughly mix it with the other rice. The finished rice will not look or feel like the rice we normally eat. Properly cooked rice for sake will be translucent with no white flecks, be very firm when chewed, and feel rubbery (but not overly sticky or mushy) to the touch. Be careful of oversteaming. It is generally better to understeam the rice than oversteam it.

Transfer the rice in its cloth package to a flat surface and spread it out to cool. When just barely warm to the touch, the rice is ready to be used.

Master Sake Recipe #2 (Advanced)

MAKES 1 GALLON

This more advanced sake recipe adds the koji, water, and rice in careful increments and spreads the initial brewing stages over several days. The yeast is fed gradually, making it stronger while also slowing down the fermentation. It's like a series of progressive small meals for the yeast instead of one big gorging feast. The result is a cleaner-tasting sake with more nuanced flavors.

A debt of thanks is owed to Fred Eckhardt, who truly pioneered sake home-brewing in the United States. He was one of the first to translate traditional Japanese sake-brewing methods into a home-brewing format. My method veers a bit from both Eckhardt's instructions and the strict Japanese style for the purpose of making sake-brewing more accessible to the average homebrewer. For a more in-depth description of traditional sake-making, please seek out Eckhardt's book on the topic (see Resources, page 176).

TOTAL INGREDIENTS

10 cups / 5 pounds sake rice, short-grained rice, or sushi-grade medium-grain rice

2½ cups / 1¼ pounds koji rice (page 146, or see Resources, page 176)

1 gallon dechlorinated water (see page 14)

½ teaspoon acid blend

1 teaspoon yeast nutrient

1½ tablespoons (½ tube) liquid sake or lager yeast, or 2 teaspoons (1 packet) dry white wine yeast

EQUIPMENT

2-quart canning jar

2-gallon fermentation bucket with lid

Air lock

Measuring cups and spoons

Long-handled spoon

Stockpot

Large fine-mesh strainer

Flour sack towel

1-gallon jug

Stopper

Racking cane and tip

Siphon hose

Hose clamp

Bottle filler

10 (12-ounce) bottles, 6 (22-ounce) bottles, or 5 (750-milliliter) wine bottles

Bottle caps or wine corks

Bottle capper or wine corker

DAY 1

¾ cup / 6 ounces short-grained rice

¼ cup / 2 ounces koji rice

1¼ cups dechlorinated water

½ teaspoon acid blend

1 teaspoon yeast nutrient

1½ tablespoons (½ tube) sake or lager yeast, or 2 teaspoons (1 packet) white wine yeast

1 • Sanitize a 2-quart canning jar, a 2-gallon bucket, its lid, and an air lock.

continued

MASTER SAKE RECIPE #2 (ADVANCED), CONTINUED

2 • Soak, steam, and cool rice as described on page 140. Combine the steamed rice, koji rice, water, acid blend, yeast nutrient, and yeast in the canning jar, and cover the jar with a piece of plastic wrap secured with a rubber band. Place the jar inside the bucket, snap on the lid, and attach the air lock. Stir the rice mash 12 hours later with a sanitized spoon.

DAYS 2 TO 6

3 • Stir the rice mash daily with a sanitized spoon. At first, the rice will swell and the mash will be almost too thick to stir. It will gradually develop a porridgelike consistency and become increasingly bubbly. Keep the mash at a steady room temperature of around 75°F.

DAY 7

¼ cup plus 3 tablespoons / 3½ ounces koji rice

1½ cups dechlorinated water

1¼ cups / 10 ounces short-grained rice

4 • Add the koji and the water to the rice mash. (Adding the koji to the mash before beginning the rice gives it time to start fermenting before the new rice is added.)

5 • Soak, steam, and cool rice as described on page 140. Stir this rice into the rice mash. If the canning jar is too small, sanitize the fermentation bucket and transfer the mash to the bucket. Place the mash somewhere cool, ideally around 55°F. Higher fermentation temperatures are okay but will yield stronger-tasting sake.

DAYS 8 TO 9

6 • Stir the mash daily with a sanitized spoon.

DAY 10

½ cup plus 3 tablespoons / 5½ ounces koji rice

4¼ cups dechlorinated water

3 cups / 1½ pounds short-grained rice

7 • Add the koji and the water to the rice mash.

8 • Soak, steam, and cool rice as described on page 140. If you have not already done so, pour the rice mash into the sanitized 2-gallon bucket. Stir in this steamed rice. Continue storing the mash somewhere cool, ideally around 55°F.

DAY 11

1 cup plus 2 tablespoons / 9 ounces koji rice

9 cups dechlorinated water

5 cups / 2½ pounds short-grained rice

9 • Add the koji and the water to the rice mash.

10 • Soak, steam, and cool rice as described on page 140. Stir this steamed rice into the mash. At this point, all the ingredients for the sake have been added to the mash.

OVER THE NEXT 2 WEEKS

11 • Maintain a cool fermentation temperature, ideally 55°F. Stir the mash daily with a sanitized spoon.

12 • You may still see signs of active fermentation after 2 weeks have passed. At this point, the sake usually has a good balance of sweet and sour flavors. You can stop fermentation now or continue fermenting for another week or two. The sake will gradually become less sweet and more sour.

TO FINISH THE SAKE

13 • Sanitize a strainer, flour sack towel, stockpot, funnel, a 1-gallon jug, and its stopper.

14 • First, pour the sake through the strainer into the stockpot. Discard all the rice solids. Set the funnel in the 1-gallon jug and line it with the flour sack towel. Strain the sake again, this time into the jug. Because of all the rice sediment, this can take a few hours. Stir the liquid in the funnel frequently to prevent the sediment from compacting and slowing down straining. If the flour sack towel becomes clogged, rinse it out, sanitize it, and replace.

15 • Clean the stockpot. Set the jug of sake, uncovered, inside the pot and fill the pot with water until the water is level with the surface of the sake. Set the pot over medium heat. Warm the sake to 140°F to pasteurize the sake and stop the koji and yeast activity (this does not affect the alcohol content). Allow the sake to cool.

16 • For nigori-style "cloudy" sake, sanitize ten 12-ounce bottles or six 22-ounce bottles (or five 750-milliliter wine bottles), their caps (or corks), the siphon hose, the racking

ALCOHOL IN SAKE

Since the koji (making the sugar) and the yeast (eating the sugar) work side-by-side when brewing sake, it's difficult to accurately gauge the final alcohol content of sake. Most home-brewed sakes are 18 to 20 percent ABV by the end of fermentation.

cane, its tip, and the bottle filler. Shake the jug of sake to make sure the sediment is fully suspended in the sake during bottling. Siphon the sake into the bottles, shaking the jug again if the sediment begins to settle. Cap (or cork) the bottles and label. Sake can be drunk immediately or aged for up to 1 year. Shake the bottle before serving and serve chilled or at room temperature.

17 • For clear sake, sanitize the stopper and air lock. Insert the stopper and air lock into the jug containing the pasteurized and cooled sake, and store the sake somewhere cool and dark for several days, during which time any remaining rice sediment will settle to the bottom of the jug.

18 • To bottle, sanitize ten 12-ounce bottles or six 22-ounce bottles (or five 750-milliliter wine bottles), their caps (or corks), the siphon hose, the racking cane, its tip, and the bottle filler. Siphon the sake into sanitized bottles, holding the tip of the racking cane just above the surface of the sediment. Cap (or cork) the bottles and label.

19 • Store the bottles in a cool, dark place for 2 weeks or up to 1 year. Serve chilled.

KOJI RICE

MAKES 2½ CUPS / 1¼ POUNDS KOJI RICE, ENOUGH FOR 1 GALLON OF SAKE (CAN BE DOUBLED)

Koji is a finicky thing to make. It requires a little tenacity and elbow grease, but it can be done in a home kitchen. The ideal situation would be to rig up a temperature-controlled container to keep the rice comfy while the koji mold takes up residence. If you'd prefer a more low-tech approach, wrapping the container of rice in towels and storing it in a picnic cooler with hot water bottles does an admirable job at keeping the rice and the koji happy. (You can also just purchase premade koji; see Resources, page 176.)

INGREDIENTS

2 cups / 1 pound sake rice, short-grained rice, or sushi-grade medium-grain rice
½ teaspoon flour or cornstarch
1 teaspoon koji spores

EQUIPMENT

Small fine-mesh plastic strainer
Flour sack towel or cheesecloth
Large plastic or glass container with a lid
Several glass bottles with lids, hot water bottle, or heating pad
Bath towel

1 • Soak, steam, and cool rice as described on page 140.

2 • Meanwhile, toast the flour or cornstarch in a small skillet over medium-high heat until it becomes fragrant, about 1 minute. This kills any wild yeast in the flour that might otherwise contaminate the koji. The flour itself will help disperse the koji spores more evenly over the rice.

3 • When the rice is just barely warm to the touch, mix the toasted flour and koji spores. Using a fine-mesh strainer, sprinkle about one-third of the powder over the rice. Lightly toss the rice with your hands to mix the grains. Add the remaining powder in two more additions, stirring the rice in between.

4 • Gather the inoculated rice in the middle of the flour sack towel used for steaming and lift it into a container big enough to hold it comfortably. Fold the edges of the cloth over the top and rest the container's lid on top. Don't actually seal the container as you want some airflow.

5 • Wrap the container with the rice in a clean towel and place it somewhere insulated that can be sealed, like a picnic cooler or even the microwave. Fill water bottles or glass jars with very hot water, seal them, and tuck them in the folds of the towel. Replace the hot water bottles every few hours.

6 • For the next 24 hours, it's important to keep the rice warm and moist. The ideal temperature for koji rice is around 95°F, though the mold will grow at temperatures

as low as 90°F and start to suffer at temperatures higher than 105°F. This temperature range is not only ideal for koji growth, but it creates the best enzymes for later in the sake-brewing process.

7 • Every 12 hours, lift the rice out of the container and open the cloth bundle to check the rice. Stir the rice with clean hands and replace it in the container.

8 • After 24 hours, you should start to notice white fuzz growing on the grains and a funky cheeselike aroma. The grains will also start to taste sweet. This is the koji spore beginning to grow on the rice and convert the rice starches to sugar. The rice will also start generating its own heat, so remove the water bottles and begin monitoring the temperature closely so it doesn't rise above 105°F. If necessary, stir the rice more frequently to cool it down and keep the temperature steady.

9 • The koji rice will be ready 40 to 54 hours after initial inoculation with the koji spore. It's finished when the white fuzz covers the grains uniformly and has penetrated roughly halfway to the core of the grain. You can check this by breaking a grain in half and judging how far the white has spread into the middle. If the grains start to turn dark tan or greenish, this is a sign that they are entering the next phase of sporulation; they are still fine to use, but should be cooled and refrigerated immediately.

10 • Spread the finished koji rice on a baking sheet to cool, then store in a sealed container for up to 2 weeks in the refrigerator or up to 3 months in the freezer.

Cloudy Cherry Sake

MAKES 1 GALLON

This may just be the prettiest sake you'll ever drink. Nigori is a style of unfiltered "cloudy" sake, so named because the rice sediment left in the sake turns it milky white in the glass. Or, in the case of this sweet cherry sake, the creamy pink of cherry blossoms. Since the sediment settles over time, you'll need to give the bottle a quick snow-globe shake before pouring.

1½ pounds fresh or frozen sweet cherries

1 gallon dechlorinated water (see page 14)

1 Campden tablet

10 cups / 5 pounds short-grain rice

2½ cups / 1¼ pounds koji rice (page 146, or see Resources, page 176)

1 teaspoon yeast nutrient

½ teaspoon acid blend

½ teaspoon pectic enzyme

1½ tablespoons (⅛ tube) liquid sake or lager yeast, or 2 teaspoons (1 packet) white wine yeast

1 • Starting 24 hours before you plan to brew, sanitize a 2-gallon bucket, its lid, the air lock, and a spoon for stirring.

2 • Pit and coarsely chop the cherries. Combine the cherries with the water in the bucket. Crush the Campden tablet and stir it in. Snap on the lid and attach the air lock. Wait 24 hours for the Campden to sterilize the cherries.

3 • The next day, soak, steam, and cool rice as described on page 140. Add the steamed rice, koji rice, yeast nutrient, acid blend, pectic enzyme, and yeast to the bucket with the cherries. (If you are steaming your rice in batches, combine everything with the first batch and add the remaining rice to the fermenter as it is cooled and ready.) Stir vigorously to distribute the yeast and aerate the rice mash.

4 • Snap on the lid and attach the air lock. Store the sake somewhere cool and dark, ideally around 55°F. You should see active fermentation as evidenced by bubbles in the air lock within 48 hours. Ferment the sake for 2 weeks, stirring daily with a sanitized spoon.

5 • To finish the sake, sanitize a strainer, flour sack towel, stockpot, funnel, a 1-gallon jug, and its stopper.

6 • First, pour the sake through the strainer into the stockpot. Discard all the rice and cherry solids. Set the funnel in the 1-gallon jug and line it with the flour sack towel.

continued

CLOUDY CHERRY SAKE, CONTINUED

Strain the sake again, this time into the jug. Because of all the rice sediment, this can take a while. Stir the liquid in the funnel frequently to prevent the sediment from compacting and slowing down the straining. If the flour sack towel becomes clogged, rinse it out, sanitize it, and replace.

7 • Clean the stockpot. Set the jug of sake, uncovered, inside the pot and fill the pot with water until the water is level with the surface of the sake. Set the pot over medium heat. Warm the sake to 140°F to pasteurize the sake and stop the koji and yeast activity (this does not affect the alcohol content). Allow the sake to cool.

8 • To bottle the sake, sanitize ten 12-ounce bottles or six 22-ounce bottles (or five 750-milliliter wine bottles), their caps (or corks), the siphon hose, the racking cane, its tip, and the bottle filler. Shake the jug of sake to make sure the sediment is fully suspended in the sake during bottling. Siphon the sake into the bottles, shaking the jug again if the sediment begins to settle. Cap (or cork) the bottles and label.

9 • Sake can be drunk immediately or aged for up to 1 year. Shake the bottles before serving and serve chilled.

ADJUSTING THE FINISHED SAKE

Homebrewed sake can taste fairly strong in the end, with the high alcohol content and sour acidity masking its more subtle fruity flavors. If you find this to be the case, you can dilute the sake to taste with dechlorinated water. Add a little at a time and taste between each addition until you like the flavor. You can also dissolve a little sugar into the sake (after pasteurization) to sweeten. Start with 1/4 cup white granulated sugar dissolved in 1/2 cup of warmed sake in a sanitized measuring cup. Mix this back into the jug of sake, taste, and repeat with more dissolved sugar as needed until the sake tastes sweet enough for you.

Also, note that homebrewed sake is naturally yellow in color. You didn't do anything wrong! Commercial sake is colorless only because it uses higher-quality milled rice not available to homebrewers, and because it is usually filtered.

Jasmine Green Tea Sake

MAKES 1 GALLON

Sake is great for sipping all on its own, of course. But it's also just begging for a play date. Infusing sake with herbs and spices is an easy—and superfun—way to begin exploring its flavor potential. I love tea infusions, and I find that the gentle floral flavor of jasmine tea is a particularly good match with the fruitiness of homebrewed sake.

1 gallon Master Sake Recipe #1 (page 138) or Master Sake Recipe #2 (page 143), pasteurized and cleared of sediment

6 bags jasmine green tea, or 1½ tablespoons loose jasmine green tea

1 • Transfer the sake into a cleaned and sanitized 1-gallon jug. Add the tea. Insert a sanitized stopper and air lock, and store in a cool, dark place for 1 to 3 weeks. Shake the jug daily to distribute the ingredients. Taste the sake occasionally; the longer you let the tea infuse, the stronger the flavor.

2 • When the sake has infused to your liking, it is ready to be bottled. Sanitize ten 12-ounce bottles or six 22-ounce bottles (or five 750-milliliter wine bottles), their caps (or corks), the siphon hose, the racking cane, its tip, and the bottle filler. Siphon the sake into the bottles, leaving the used tea bags or loose-leaf tea behind. Cap (or cork) the bottles and label.

3 • Store the bottles in a cool, dark place for 2 weeks or up to 1 year. Serve chilled.

Meyer Lemon–Thyme Sake

MAKES 1 GALLON

Sake with a touch of citrus is a beautiful thing. I had been serving my sake with a twist of lemon peel in each cup when it occurred to me that I should just try infusing it from the get-go. Done and done. The result is this cousin to limoncello: a silky, citrusy sake with a touch of woodsy thyme. Mix it with a little sparkling water for a heavenly spring cocktail.

1 gallon Master Sake Recipe #1 (page 138) or Master Sake Recipe #2 (page 143), pasteurized and cleared of sediment

8 sprigs fresh thyme

8 Meyer lemons

1 • Transfer the sake into a cleaned and sanitized 1-gallon jug. Lightly crush the thyme with a rolling pin or the blunt side of a knife. Peel the zests off the lemons with a vegetable peeler, leaving as much of the white pith behind as possible. Save the lemons for another purpose. Add the thyme and the lemon zest to the sake. Insert a sanitized stopper and air lock, and store in a cool, dark place for 1 to 3 weeks. Shake the jug daily to distribute the ingredients. Taste the sake occasionally; the longer you let the ingredients infuse, the stronger the flavors.

2 • When the sake has infused to your liking, it is ready to be bottled. Sanitize ten 12-ounce bottles or six 22-ounce bottles (or five 750-milliliter wine bottles), their caps (or corks), the siphon hose, the racking cane, its tip, and the bottle filler. Siphon the sake into the bottles, leaving the thyme and lemon peels behind. Cap (or cork) the bottles and label.

3 • Store the bottles in a cool, dark place for 2 weeks or up to 1 year. Serve chilled.

Gin-Infused Sake

MAKES 1 GALLON

No distilling required for this gin. Just a fresh batch of sake and a handful of herbs and spices. Juniper berries are the top flavoring component of gin, and here they give the sake a pungent pine-like flavor. You'll find them at specialty spice stores, like Penzeys Spices (see Resources, page 176).

1 gallon Master Sake Recipe #1 (page 138) or Master Sake Recipe #2 (page 143), pasteurized and cleared of sediment

½ cup dried juniper berries

4 teaspoons coriander seed

1 teaspoon allspice berries

1 teaspoon fennel seeds

15 cardamom pods, cracked open with a rolling pin

½ teaspoon black peppercorns

1 bay leaf

3 sprigs fresh rosemary

Zest from 12 lemons

1 • Transfer the sake into cleaned and sanitized 1-gallon jug. Add the juniper berries. Insert a sanitized stopper and air lock, and store in a cool, dark place. Infuse for 12 hours, then add the coriander seed, allspice, fennel seed, cardamom pods, peppercorns, bay leaf, rosemary, and lemon zest. Infuse for another 12 to 24 hours. Taste the sake occasionally during this time; the longer you let the ingredients infuse, the stronger the flavors.

2 • When the sake has infused to your liking, it is ready to bottle. Sanitize ten 12-ounce bottles or six 22-ounce bottles (or five 750-milliliter wine bottles), their caps (or corks), the siphon hose, the racking cane, its tip, and the bottle filler. Siphon the sake into the bottles, leaving the used spices behind. Cap (or cork) the bottles and label.

3 • Store the bottles in a cool, dark place for 2 weeks or up to 1 year. Serve chilled.

CHAPTER 8

Fruit Wine

EXPERT INTERVIEW

Glenn Foster, head winemaker and owner, Talon Wine Brands, Palisade, Colorado

How did Talon Wine Brands start making fruit wines?

When you're out peddling wine, everyone's got a Chardonnay and everyone's got a Merlot. But no one has a cherry or a pomegranate or a strawberry-rhubarb. Fruit wines are the unusual commodity. We have something that nobody else has, and I like that.

What is your wine-making philosophy?

We want the wine to taste like the fruit that it came from. A lot of people will look down on fruit wines and crinkle up their noses. But when they taste them, and the peach actually tastes like peaches and the strawberry-rhubarb actually tastes like grandma's pie, that's awesome.

What is the trickiest part of making fruit wines?

One of the things that we've discovered is that it helps to keep the fermentation cool, even though that can be difficult sometimes. We try to keep it below 55°F. That's a little hard on the yeast, but helps to preserve the fruity character of the wine and doesn't strip the aromas as much.

What is different about making fruit wines as opposed to grape wines?

After you ferment the fruit wine, you lose a lot of the actual essence and character of the fruit. It will taste slightly like peaches, for instance, but there's not really a lot of peach character once the wine is done fermenting. Those essential fruit aromas are very volatile and float away during the fermentation process. So we'll add some juice after it has finished fermenting to bring back the character.

What is one thing homebrewers could do to improve their wines?

Just put yourself in the yeasts' shoes. Make them happy. Making wine is like treating yeast to a day spa: sing to them, give them foot massages, do their nails. We do a whole bunch of things just to make the yeast feel comfortable. Recognize that these are living creatures, and they have certain requirements.

TALON WINES TO TRY: St. Kathryn Cellars Lavender, Strawberry Rhubarb, Cranberry Kiss

Master Wine Recipe

MAKES 1 GALLON

Making wine is remarkably, and blessedly, straightforward. All you need to do is mix sugar with water and a boatload of fresh fruit, and then add yeast. Strain, age, bottle, and then age some more, and you will be rewarded a few months later with the purest essence of whatever fruit you originally used. It's practically guaranteed to be delicious. For all the hoopla made over wine, you'd think it would be more difficult to make. (And having said that, you will note that I do not even touch upon grape wines in this book. That is a complex topic best left for both the experts and another time. You can certainly feel free to play around with grapes using this recipe, particularly if you have access to actual wine grapes. Just know that it won't taste quite as robust or fully flavored as the grape wines you're used to.)

Your aim is to make a gallon of wine, so base your initial measurements of water and fruit on making a gallon total of liquid. With very juicy fruits like peaches and melon, use less water; with fleshy fruits like blueberries, use more. Remember you will be straining out the fruit solids later. This all takes a little guesswork, and it's fine if you come in a little over or under a gallon. You can always add more water later to make a gallon, and the recipe will still work just fine if you're a little over.

Add sugar based on the sweetness of your fruit (or lack thereof) and acid blend to balance out fruits with little natural acidity. Ditto with adding tannin. Err on the side of caution to begin with since you can always add more of these ingredients once you taste the wine down the road.

INGREDIENTS

12 to 16 cups water

2¼ cups to 6¾ cups / 1 to 3 pounds white granulated sugar

3 to 4 pounds fruit

2 Campden tablets

2 teaspoons (1 packet) dry wine yeast

1 teaspoon yeast nutrient

Up to 2 teaspoons acid blend (optional)

½ teaspoon pectic enzyme

⅛ to ½ teaspoon tannin

EQUIPMENT

Stockpot

Measuring cups and spoons

Long-handled spoon

2-gallon fermentation bucket with lid

Air lock

Hydrometer

Mesh bag

1-quart canning jar

Large fine-mesh strainer

Flour sack towel or cheesecloth

Funnel

1-gallon jug

Stopper

Racking cane and tip

Siphon hose

Hose clamp

Bottle filler

10 (12-ounce) bottles, 6 (22-ounce) bottles, or 5 (750-milliliter) wine bottles

Bottle caps or wine corks

Bottle capper or corker

1 • Sanitize a 2-gallon bucket, its lid, the air lock, and a spoon for stirring.

2 • Bring the water to a simmer in a stockpot over medium-high heat and stir in the sugar. Stir just until the sugar dissolves and then remove from heat. Let stand until cooled to room temperature.

3 • Pour the sugar water into the 2-gallon bucket. Coarsely chop the fruit into bite-size pieces (berries and small fruits can be kept whole), secure in a mesh bag, and add to the liquid. Using a potato masher or very clean hands, mash the submerged bag of fruit to extract as much juice as possible. Take a hydrometer reading to determine the original gravity (see Brewer's Handbook, page 16). Crush 1 Campden tablet and stir it in. Snap on the lid and attach the air lock. Wait 24 hours for the Campden to sterilize the fruit.

4 • After the fruit is sterilized, prepare the yeast starter. Sanitize a measuring cup, a 1-quart canning jar, and a stirring spoon. Scoop out 1 cup of the fruity liquid and pour it into the canning jar. Pour the yeast over top and cover the jar with a piece of plastic wrap secured with a rubber band. Give the jar a good shake and let it stand for 1 to 3 hours. It should become foamy, and you will see tiny bubbles popping on the surface of the liquid. Once you see some sign of activity, the yeast starter can be used. (See Brewer's Handbook, page 15.)

5 • Pour the starter into the fermentation bucket along with the yeast nutrient, acid blend, pectic enzyme, and ⅛ teaspoon tannin. Stir vigorously to distribute the yeast and aerate the liquid. Snap the lid back on and reattach the air lock. You should see active fermentation as evidenced by bubbles in the air lock within 48 hours.

6 • Let the wine ferment for 1 week, stirring daily with a sanitized spoon. After this time, the wine is ready to transfer into a 1-gallon jug for the secondary fermentation.

7 • Sanitize a 1-gallon jug, its stopper, a strainer, a funnel, a flour sack towel or cheesecloth, and a long-handled spoon. Pull out the bag of fruit with clean hands and squeeze gently to extract as much liquid as possible.

8 • Insert the funnel into the 1-gallon jug and line it with the cloth. Slowly pour the wine into the jug, filtering out the solids. Use the spoon as necessary to stir up the sediment that collects in the funnel. Seal the jug with its stopper and insert the air lock.

continued

MASTER WINE RECIPE, CONTINUED

9 • Let the wine sit somewhere cool and dark for 4 weeks. By this point, you should see no real signs of fermentation. Watch the air lock: if 2 minutes pass without seeing any bubbles, fermentation is essentially complete. You can bottle the wine now or continue aging it for up to 6 months.

10 • If you are continuing to age, it's good to occasionally rack (siphon) the wine off the sediment that collects on the bottom of the jug. Sanitize a stockpot, the siphon hose, the racking cane, and its tip. Siphon the wine into the stockpot. Clean and sanitize the jug, stopper, and air lock, and siphon the wine back into the jug. Insert the stopper and air lock. This also provides a good opportunity to taste the wine and see how it's coming along. If it tastes a little sweet, you can add extra acid blend to give it some tartness or some tannin for dryness and astringency. Start with a little of these ingredients, taste after a week or two, and continue adjusting as needed. The wine can be bottled whenever it tastes good to you.

11 • When ready to bottle, sanitize a stockpot, the siphon hose, the racking cane, and its tip. Siphon the wine into the stockpot, crush the remaining Campden tablet, and stir it into the wine. Clean and sanitize the jug, stopper, and air lock, and siphon the wine back into the jug. Insert the stopper and air lock. Wait at least 24 hours before bottling.

12 • To bottle the wine, sanitize ten 12-ounce bottles or six 22-ounce bottles (or five 750-milliliter wine bottles), their caps (or corks), the siphon hose, the racking cane, its tip, and the bottle filler. Siphon ½ cup of wine to the hydrometer and use to determine final gravity. Drink the wine or pour it back into the jug once used. Siphon the wine into the bottles, cap (or cork), and label.

13 • Store the bottles in a cool, dark place for 2 weeks or up to 1 year. Serve chilled or at room temperature.

Plum Wine

MAKES 1 GALLON
TARGET ORIGINAL GRAVITY RANGE = 1.115–1.120
TARGET FINAL GRAVITY RANGE = 1.000–1.005
TARGET ABV = 16.5 PERCENT

Much depends on the plums you choose for this wine. Tart plums will give you a crisp and light wine that could be distant cousin to a Pinot Grigio. Sweet juicy plums picked at the height of summer will give you something closer to a dessert wine. Go for a mix and—you guessed it!—you'll find yourself with a medium-bodied wine somewhere between the two. Truly, there are no wrong choices here.

12 cups water

5⅔ cups / 2½ pounds white granulated sugar

4 pounds plums

2 Campden tablets

2 teaspoons (1 packet) dry white wine yeast

2 teaspoons acid blend

1 teaspoon yeast nutrient

½ teaspoon pectic enzyme

⅛ teaspoon tannin

1 • Sanitize a 2-gallon bucket, its lid, the air lock, and a spoon for stirring.

2 • Bring the water to a simmer and stir in the sugar. Stir just until the sugar dissolves, then remove from heat. Let stand until cooled to room temperature.

3 • Pour the sugar water into the 2-gallon bucket. Coarsely chop the plums, discarding the pits. Secure the fruit in a mesh bag and add to the liquid. Using a potato masher or very clean hands, mash the submerged bag of fruit to extract as much juice as possible. Take a hydrometer reading to determine the original gravity (see Brewer's Handbook, page 16). Crush 1 Campden tablet and stir it in. Snap on the lid and attach the air lock. Wait 24 hours for the Campden to sterilize the fruit.

4 • After the plums are sterilized, prepare the yeast starter. Sanitize a measuring cup, a 1-canning quart jar, and a stirring spoon. Scoop out 1 cup of the fruity liquid and pour it into the canning jar. Pour the yeast over top and cover the jar with a piece of plastic wrap secured with a rubber band. Give the jar a good shake and let it stand for 1 to 3 hours. It should become foamy, and you will see tiny bubbles popping on the surface of the liquid. Once you see some sign of activity, the starter can be used.

continued

PLUM WINE, CONTINUED

5 • Pour the starter into the fermentation bucket along with the acid blend, yeast nutrient, pectic enzyme, and tannin. Stir vigorously to distribute the yeast and aerate the wine. Snap the lid back on and reattach the air lock. You should see active fermentation as evidenced by bubbles in the air lock within 48 hours.

6 • Let the wine ferment for 1 week, stirring daily with a sanitized spoon. After this time, the wine is ready to transfer into a 1-gallon jug for the secondary fermentation.

7 • Sanitize a 1-gallon jug, its stopper, a strainer, a funnel, a flour sack towel or cheesecloth, and a long-handled spoon. Pull out the bag of plums with clean hands and squeeze gently to extract as much liquid as possible.

8 • Insert the funnel into the 1-gallon jug and line it with the cloth. Slowly pour the wine into the jug, filtering out the solids. Use the spoon as necessary to stir up the sediment that collects in the funnel. Seal the jug with its stopper and insert the air lock.

9 • Let the wine sit somewhere cool and dark for 4 weeks. You can bottle the wine now or continue aging it for up to 6 months.

10 • If you are continuing to age, it's good to occasionally rack the wine off the sediment that collects on the bottom of the jug.

Sanitize a stockpot, the siphon hose, the racking cane, and its tip. Siphon the wine into the stockpot. Clean and sanitize the jug, stopper, air lock, and siphon the wine back into the jug. Insert the stopper and air lock. You can sample the wine and adjust the acid or tannins to your taste during this step.

11 • When ready to bottle, sanitize a stockpot, the siphon hose, the racking cane, and its tip. Siphon the wine into a sanitized stockpot, crush the remaining Campden tablet, and stir it into the wine. Clean and sanitize the jug, stopper, and air lock, and siphon the wine back into the jug. Insert the stopper and air lock. Wait at least 24 hours before bottling.

12 • To bottle the wine, sanitize ten 12-ounce bottles or six 22-ounce bottles (or five 750-milliliter wine bottles), their caps (or corks), the siphon hose, the racking cane, its tip, and the bottle filler. Siphon ½ cup of wine to the hydrometer and use to determine final gravity. Drink the wine or pour it back into the jug once used. Siphon the wine into the bottles, cap (or cork), and label.

13 • Store the bottles in a cool, dark place for 2 weeks or up to 1 year. Serve chilled.

Strawberry Wine

MAKES 1 GALLON
TARGET ORIGINAL GRAVITY RANGE = 1.085–1.090
TARGET FINAL GRAVITY RANGE = 1.000–1.005
TARGET ABV = 12.5 PERCENT

Throw away any preconceptions you might have about strawberry wine being syrupy, overly sweet, or otherwise gag inducing. Banish the words "lips like strawberry wine" from your vernacular. Instead, think of those tiny strawberries, just picked and still warm from the sun, which burst in your mouth and deliver the perfect package of tart-sweet strawberry essence. This is real strawberry wine. Accept no imitations.

13 cups water
4½ cups / 2 pounds white granulated sugar
4 pounds fresh strawberries
2 Campden tablets
2 teaspoons (1 packet) dry white wine yeast
2 teaspoons acid blend
1 teaspoon yeast nutrient
½ teaspoon pectic enzyme
⅛ teaspoon tannin

1 • Sanitize a 2-gallon bucket, its lid, the air lock, and a spoon for stirring.

2 • Bring the water to a simmer and stir in the sugar. Stir just until the sugar dissolves and then remove from heat. Let stand until cooled to room temperature.

3 • Pour the sugar water into the 2-gallon bucket. Hull and coarsely chop the strawberries, secure them in a mesh bag, and add to the liquid. Using a potato masher or very clean hands, mash the submerged bag of fruit to extract as much juice as possible. Take a hydrometer reading to determine the original gravity (see Brewer's Handbook, page 16). Crush 1 Campden tablet and stir it in. Snap on the lid and attach the air lock. Wait 24 hours for the Campden to sterilize the fruit.

4 • After the strawberries are sterilized, prepare the yeast starter. Sanitize a measuring cup, a 1-quart canning jar, and a stirring spoon. Scoop out 1 cup of the fruity liquid and pour it into the canning jar. Pour the yeast over top and cover the jar with a piece of plastic wrap secured with a rubber band. Give the jar a good shake and let it stand for 1 to 3 hours. It should become foamy, and you will see tiny bubbles popping on the surface of the liquid. Once you see some sign of activity, the starter can be used.

5 • Pour the starter into the fermentation bucket along with the acid blend, yeast nutrient, pectic enzyme, and tannin. Stir vigorously to distribute the yeast and aerate the wine. Snap the lid back on and reattach the air lock. You should see active fermentation as evidenced by bubbles in the air lock within 48 hours.

6 • Let the wine ferment for 1 week, stirring daily with a sanitized spoon. After this time, the wine is ready to transfer into a 1-gallon jug for the secondary fermentation.

7 • Sanitize a 1-gallon jug, its stopper, a strainer, a funnel, a flour sack towel or cheesecloth, and a long-handled spoon. Pull out the bag of strawberries with clean hands and squeeze gently to extract as much liquid as possible.

8 • Insert the funnel into the 1-gallon jug and line it with the cloth. Slowly pour the wine into the jug, filtering out the solids. Use the spoon as necessary to stir up the sediment that collects in the funnel. Seal the jug with its stopper and insert the air lock.

9 • Let the wine sit somewhere cool and dark for 4 weeks. You can bottle the wine now or continue aging it for up to 6 months.

10 • If you are continuing to age, it's good to occasionally rack the wine off the sediment that collects on the bottom of the jug. Sanitize a stockpot, the siphon hose, the racking cane, and its tip. Siphon the wine into the stockpot. Clean and sanitize the jug, stopper, and air lock, and siphon the wine back into the jug. Insert the stopper and air lock. You can sample the wine and adjust the acid or tannins to your taste during this step.

11 • When ready to bottle, sanitize a stockpot, the siphon hose, the racking cane, and its tip. Siphon the wine into the stockpot, crush the remaining Campden tablet, and stir it into the wine. Clean and sanitize the jug, stopper, and air lock, and siphon the wine back into the jug. Insert the stopper and air lock. Wait at least 24 hours before bottling.

12 • To bottle the wine, sanitize ten 12-ounce bottles or six 22-ounce bottles (or five 750-milliliter wine bottles), their caps (or corks), the siphon hose, the racking cane, its tip, and the bottle filler. Siphon ½ cup of wine to the hydrometer and use to determine final gravity. Drink the wine or pour it back into the jug once used. Siphon the wine into the bottles, cap (or cork), and label.

13 • Store the bottles in a cool, dark place for 2 weeks or up to 1 year. Serve chilled.

Blackberry Wine

MAKES 1 GALLON
TARGET ORIGINAL GRAVITY RANGE = 1.090–1.095
TARGET FINAL GRAVITY RANGE = 1.000–1.005
TARGET ABV = 13 PERCENT

Blackberries translate into wine with an almost magical ease. They are already tart and slightly tannic, and they have that insanely deep and luscious berry flavor that keeps us picking at the roadside bush long after our arms are scratched and stained purple. Making blackberries into wine feels like letting nature take its course.

14 cups water
4½ cups / 2 pounds white granulated sugar
3½ pounds blackberries
2 Campden tablets
2 teaspoons (1 packet) dry red wine yeast
2 teaspoons acid blend
1 teaspoon yeast nutrient
½ teaspoon pectic enzyme
½ teaspoon tannin

1 • Sanitize a 2-gallon bucket, its lid, the air lock, and a spoon for stirring.

2 • Bring the water to a simmer and stir in the sugar. Stir just until the sugar dissolves and then remove from heat. Let stand until cooled to room temperature.

3 • Pour the sugar water into the 2-gallon bucket. Secure the blackberries in a mesh bag and add them to the sugar water. Using a potato masher or very clean hands, mash the submerged bag of fruit to extract as much juice as possible. Take a hydrometer reading to determine the original gravity (see Brewer's Handbook, page 16). Crush 1 Campden tablet and stir it in. Snap on the lid and attach the air lock. Wait 24 hours for the Campden to sterilize the fruit.

4 • After the berries are sterilized, prepare the yeast starter. Sanitize a measuring cup, a 1-quart canning jar, and a stirring spoon. Scoop out 1 cup of the fruity liquid and pour it into the canning jar. Pour the yeast over top and cover the jar with a piece of plastic wrap secured with a rubber band. Give the jar a good shake and let it stand for 1 to 3 hours. It should become foamy, and you will see tiny bubbles popping on the surface of the liquid. Once you see some sign of activity, the starter can be used.

5 • Pour the starter into the fermentation bucket along with the acid blend, yeast nutrient, pectic enzyme, and tannin. Stir vigorously to distribute the yeast and aerate the wine. Snap the lid back on and reattach the air lock. You should see active fermentation as evidenced by bubbles in the air lock within 48 hours.

6 • Let the wine ferment for 1 week, stirring daily with a sanitized spoon. After this time, the wine is ready to transfer into a 1-gallon jug for the secondary fermentation.

7 • Sanitize a 1-gallon jug, its stopper, a strainer, a funnel, a flour sack towel or cheesecloth, and a long-handled spoon. Pull out the bag of blackberries with clean hands and squeeze gently to extract as much liquid as possible.

8 • Insert the funnel into the 1-gallon jug and line it with the cloth. Slowly pour the wine into the jug, filtering out the solids. Use the spoon as necessary to stir up the sediment that collects in the funnel. Seal the jug with its stopper and insert the air lock.

9 • Let the wine sit somewhere cool and dark for 4 weeks. You can bottle the wine now or continue aging it for up to 6 months.

10 • If you are continuing to age, it's good to occasionally rack the wine off the sediment that collects on the bottom of the jug. Sanitize a stockpot, the siphon hose, the racking cane, and its tip. Siphon the wine into the stockpot. Clean and sanitize the jug, stopper, and air lock, and siphon the wine back into the jug. Insert the stopper and air lock. You can sample the wine and adjust the acid or tannins to your taste during this step.

11 • When ready to bottle, sanitize a stockpot, the siphon hose, the racking cane, and its tip. Siphon the wine into a sanitized stockpot, crush the remaining Campden tablet, and stir it into the wine. Clean and sanitize the jug, stopper, and air lock, and siphon the wine back into the jug. Insert the stopper and air lock. Wait at least 24 hours before bottling.

12 • To bottle the wine, sanitize ten 12-ounce bottles or six 22-ounce bottles (or five 750-milliliter wine bottles), their caps (or corks), the siphon hose, the racking cane, its tip, and the bottle filler. Siphon ½ cup of wine to the hydrometer and use to determine final gravity. Drink the wine or pour it back into the jug once used. Siphon the wine into the bottles, cap (or cork), and label.

13 • Store the bottles in a cool, dark place for 2 weeks or up to 1 year. Serve at room temperature.

Raspberry-Rhubarb Wine

MAKES 1 GALLON
TARGET ORIGINAL GRAVITY RANGE = 1.090–1.095
TARGET FINAL GRAVITY RANGE = 1.000–1.005
TARGET ABV = 13.5 PERCENT

The classic companion to rhubarb is, of course, strawberry. You'll get no argument here. But it's the unlikely marriage of raspberry and rhubarb that really holds my affection. It works in cobblers, it works in jam, and it certainly works in wine. Make this tart and bracing wine in that brief window of seasonal opportunity when both rhubarb and raspberries are available, and then save it to toast the first days of spring the following year.

14 cups water
5⅔ cups / 2½ pounds white granulated sugar
2 pounds rhubarb stems
2 pounds fresh or frozen raspberries
2 Campden tablets
2 teaspoons (1 packet) dry white wine yeast
1 teaspoon acid blend
1 teaspoon yeast nutrient
½ teaspoon pectic enzyme
⅛ teaspoon tannin

1 • Sanitize a 2-gallon bucket, its lid, the air lock, and a spoon for stirring.

2 • Bring the water to a simmer and stir in the sugar. Stir just until the sugar dissolves and then remove from heat. Let stand until cooled to room temperature.

3 • Pour the sugar water into the 2-gallon bucket. Coarsely chop the rhubarb, secure the rhubarb pieces with the raspberries in a mesh bag, and add to the liquid. Using a potato masher or very clean hands, mash the submerged bag of fruit to extract as much juice as possible. Take a hydrometer reading to determine the original gravity (see Brewer's Handbook, page 16). Crush 1 Campden tablet and stir it in. Snap on the lid and attach the air lock. Wait 24 hours for the Campden to sterilize the fruit.

4 • After the fruit is sterilized, prepare the yeast starter. Sanitize a measuring cup, a 1-quart canning jar, and a stirring spoon. Scoop out 1 cup of the fruity liquid and pour it into the canning jar. Pour the yeast over top and cover the jar with a piece of plastic wrap secured with a rubber band. Give the jar a good shake and let it stand for 1 to 3 hours. It should become foamy, and you will see tiny bubbles popping on the surface of the liquid. Once you see some sign of activity, the starter can be used.

5 • Pour the starter into the fermentation bucket along with the acid blend, yeast nutrient, pectic enzyme, and tannin. Stir vigorously to distribute the yeast and aerate the wine. Snap the lid back on and reattach the air lock. You should see active fermentation as evidenced by bubbles in the air lock within 48 hours.

6 • Let the wine ferment for 1 week, stirring daily with a sanitized spoon. After this time, the wine is ready to transfer into a 1-gallon jug for the secondary fermentation.

7 • Sanitize a 1-gallon jug, its stopper, a strainer, a funnel, a flour sack towel or cheesecloth, and a long-handled spoon. Pull out the bag of fruit with clean hands and squeeze gently to extract as much liquid as possible.

8 • Insert the funnel into the 1-gallon jug and line it with the cloth. Slowly pour the wine into the jug, filtering out the solids. Use the spoon as necessary to stir up the sediment that collects in the funnel. Seal the jug with its stopper and insert the air lock.

9 • Let the wine sit somewhere cool and dark for 4 weeks. You can bottle the wine now or continue aging it for up to 6 months.

10 • If you are continuing to age, it's good to occasionally rack the wine off the sediment that collects on the bottom of the jug. Sanitize a stockpot, the siphon hose, the racking cane, and its tip. Siphon the wine into the stockpot. Clean and sanitize the jug, stopper, and air lock, and siphon the wine back into the jug. Insert the stopper and air lock. You can sample the wine and adjust the acid or tannins to your taste during this step.

11 • When ready to bottle, sanitize a stockpot, the siphon hose, the racking cane, and its tip. Siphon the wine into a sanitized stockpot, crush the remaining Campden tablet, and stir it into the wine. Clean and sanitize the jug, stopper, and air lock, and siphon the wine back into the jug. Insert the stopper and air lock. Wait at least 24 hours before bottling.

12 • To bottle the wine, sanitize ten 12-ounce bottles or six 22-ounce bottles (or five 750-milliliter wine bottles), their caps (or corks), the siphon hose, the racking cane, its tip, and the bottle filler. Siphon ½ cup of wine to the hydrometer and use to determine final gravity. Drink the wine or pour it back into the jug once used. Siphon the wine into the bottles, cap (or cork), and label.

13 • Store the bottles in a cool, dark place for 2 weeks or up to 1 year. Serve chilled.

Blueberry-Pomegranate Wine

MAKES 1 GALLON
TARGET ORIGINAL GRAVITY RANGE = 1.110–1.115
TARGET FINAL GRAVITY RANGE = 1.000–1.005
TARGET ABV = 16.5 PERCENT

Of all the wine recipes here, this is the most similar to classic red table wine. Blueberries are a surprisingly sweet ingredient to work with, and the pomegranate juice adds some much needed tartness and dry astringency. Together, they make a dynamic duo: aromatic, balanced, and nicely complex.

12 cups water

5⅔ cups / 2½ pounds white granulated sugar

3 pounds fresh or frozen blueberries

2 cups pomegranate juice

2 Campden tablets

2 teaspoons (1 packet) dry red wine yeast

2 teaspoons acid blend

1 teaspoon yeast nutrient

½ teaspoon pectic enzyme

½ teaspoon tannin

1 • Sanitize a 2-gallon bucket, its lid, the air lock, and a spoon for stirring.

2 • Bring the water to a simmer and stir in the sugar. Stir just until the sugar dissolves and then remove from heat. Let stand until cooled to room temperature.

3 • Pour the sugar water and pomegranate juice into the 2-gallon bucket. Secure the blueberries in a mesh bag and add to the liquid. Using a potato masher or very clean hands, mash the submerged bag of fruit to extract as much juice as possible. Take a hydrometer reading to determine the original gravity (see Brewer's Handbook, page 16). Crush 1 Campden tablet and stir it in. Snap on the lid and attach the air lock. Wait 24 hours for the Campden to sterilize the fruit.

4 • After the blueberries are sterilized, prepare the yeast starter. Sanitize a measuring cup, a 1-quart canning jar, and a stirring spoon. Scoop out 1 cup of the fruity liquid and pour it into the canning jar. Pour the yeast over top and cover the jar with a piece of plastic wrap secured with a rubber band. Give the jar a good shake and let it stand for 1 to 3 hours. It should become foamy, and you will see tiny bubbles popping on the surface of the liquid. Once you see some sign of activity, the starter can be used.

5 • Pour the starter into the fermentation bucket along with the acid blend, yeast nutrient, pectic enzyme, and tannin. Stir

continued

BLUEBERRY-POMEGRANATE WINE, CONTINUED

vigorously to distribute the yeast and aerate the wine. Snap the lid back on and reattach the air lock. You should see active fermentation as evidenced by bubbles in the air lock within 48 hours.

6 • Let the wine ferment for 1 week, stirring daily with a sanitized spoon. After this time, the wine is ready to transfer into a 1-gallon jug for the secondary fermentation.

7 • Sanitize a 1-gallon jug, its stopper, a strainer, a funnel, a flour sack towel or cheesecloth, and a long-handled spoon. Pull out the bag of blueberries with clean hands and squeeze gently to extract as much juice as possible.

8 • Insert the funnel into the 1-gallon jug and line it with the cloth. Slowly pour the wine into the jug, filtering out the solids. Use the spoon as necessary to stir up the sediment that collects in the funnel. Seal the jug with its stopper and insert the air lock.

9 • Let the wine sit somewhere cool and dark for 4 weeks. You can bottle the wine now or continue aging it for up to 6 months.

10 • If you are continuing to age, it's good to occasionally rack the wine off the sediment that collects on the bottom of the jug. Sanitize a stockpot, the siphon hose, the racking cane, and its tip. Siphon the wine into the stockpot. Clean and sanitize the jug, stopper, and air lock, and siphon the wine back into the jug. Insert the stopper and air lock. You can sample the wine and adjust the acid or tannins to your taste during this step.

11 • When ready to bottle, sanitize a stockpot, the siphon hose, the racking cane, and its tip. Siphon the wine into the stockpot, crush the remaining Campden tablet, and stir it into the wine. Clean and sanitize the jug, stopper, and air lock, and siphon the wine back into the jug. Insert the stopper and air lock. Wait at least 24 hours before bottling.

12 • To bottle the wine, sanitize ten 12-ounce bottles or six 22-ounce bottles (or five 750-milliliter wine bottles), their caps (or corks), the siphon hose, the racking cane, its tip, and the bottle filler. Siphon ½ cup of wine to the hydrometer and use to determine final gravity. Drink the wine or pour it back into the jug once used. Siphon the wine into the bottles, cap (or cork), and label.

13 • Store the bottles in a cool, dark place for 2 weeks or up to 1 year. Serve at room temperature.

Summer Melon Wine

MAKES 1 GALLON
TARGET ORIGINAL GRAVITY RANGE = 1.090–1.095
TARGET FINAL GRAVITY RANGE = 1.000–1.005
TARGET ABV = 13.5 PERCENT

Okay, yes. A wine made from cantaloupe sounds rather weird. I thought so myself, but I also couldn't get the idea out of my head. Would it taste like that first syrupy bite taken from a half moon of perfectly ripe melon? Or more like nibbling too close to the rind? As it turns out, it tastes like a bit of both. If you're looking for a wine to truly shock and awe your fan club, this is the one.

12 cups water
5⅔ cups / 2½ pounds white granulated sugar
6½ pounds whole cantaloupe
2 Campden tablets
2 teaspoons (1 package) dry champagne yeast
2 teaspoons acid blend
1 teaspoon yeast nutrient
½ teaspoon pectic enzyme
⅛ teaspoon tannin

1 • Sanitize a 2-gallon bucket, its lid, the air lock, and a spoon for stirring.

2 • Bring the water to a simmer and stir in the sugar. Stir just until the sugar dissolves and then remove from heat. Let stand until cooled to room temperature.

3 • Pour the sugar water into the 2-gallon bucket. Coarsely chop the cantaloupe, discarding the rinds and the seeds, secure in a mesh bag, and add to the liquid. Using a potato masher or very clean hands, mash the submerged bag of fruit to extract as much juice as possible. Take a hydrometer reading to determine the original gravity (see Brewer's Handbook, page 16). Crush 1 Campden tablet and stir it in. Snap on the lid and attach the air lock. Wait 24 hours for the Campden to sterilize the fruit.

4 • After the cantaloupe is sterilized, prepare the yeast starter. Sanitize a measuring cup, a 1-quart canning jar, and a stirring spoon. Scoop out 1 cup of the fruity liquid and pour it into the canning jar. Pour the yeast over top and cover the jar with a piece of plastic wrap secured with a rubber band. Give the jar a good shake and let it stand for 1 to 3 hours. It should become foamy, and you will see tiny bubbles popping on the surface of the liquid. Once you see some sign of activity, the starter can be used.

5 • Pour the starter into the fermentation bucket along with the acid blend, yeast nutrient, pectic enzyme, and tannin. Stir

continued

SUMMER MELON WINE, CONTINUED

vigorously to distribute the yeast and aerate the wine. Snap the lid back on and reattach the air lock. You should see active fermentation as evidenced by bubbles in the air lock within 48 hours.

6 • Let the wine ferment for 1 week, stirring daily with a sanitized spoon. After this time, the wine is ready to transfer into a 1-gallon jug for the secondary fermentation.

7 • Sanitize a 1-gallon jug, its stopper, a strainer, a funnel, a flour sack towel or cheesecloth, and a long-handled spoon. Pull out the bag of melon with clean hands and squeeze gently to extract as much liquid as possible.

8 • Insert the funnel into the 1-gallon jug and line it with the cloth. Slowly pour the wine into the jug, filtering out the solids. Use the spoon as necessary to stir up the sediment that collects in the funnel. Seal the jug with its stopper and insert the air lock.

9 • Let the wine sit somewhere cool and dark for another 4 weeks. You can bottle the wine now or continue aging it for up to 6 months.

10 • If you are continuing to age, it's good to occasionally rack the wine off the sediment that collects on the bottom of the jug. Sanitize a stockpot, the siphon hose, the racking cane, and its tip. Siphon the wine into the stockpot. Clean and sanitize the jug, stopper, and air lock, and siphon the wine back into the jug. Insert the stopper and air lock. You can sample the wine and adjust the acid or tannins to your taste during this step.

11 • When ready to bottle, sanitize a stockpot, the siphon hose, the racking cane, and its tip. Siphon the wine into the stockpot, crush the remaining Campden tablet, and stir it into the wine. Clean and sanitize the jug, stopper, and air lock, and siphon the wine back into the jug. Insert the stopper and air lock. Wait at least 24 hours before bottling.

12 • To bottle the wine, sanitize ten 12-ounce bottles or six 22-ounce bottles (or five 750-milliliter wine bottles), their caps (or corks), the siphon hose, the racking cane, its tip, and the bottle filler. Siphon ½ cup of wine to the hydrometer and use to determine final gravity. Drink the wine or pour it back into the jug once used. Siphon the wine into the bottles, cap (or cork), and label.

13 • Store the bottles in a cool, dark place for 2 weeks or up to 1 year. Serve chilled or at room temperature.

Sparkling Sour Cherry Wine

MAKES 1 GALLON
TARGET ORIGINAL GRAVITY RANGE = 1.070–1.075
TARGET FINAL GRAVITY RANGE = 1.000–1.005
TARGET ABV = 10 PERCENT

You want to get a party started? Serve this wine. It's bubbly and exciting and will, without fail, start a conversation—one that's mostly along the lines of, "Holy cow, you really made this?" I recommend practicing your gracious and sagelike nod ahead of time. If you like, include the pits with the cherries for a nutty cherry-wood flavor. The pits do contain some arsenic, but since they are left whole and a relatively small number is used, they will not adversely affect the wine or your constitution.

14 cups water

2¼ cups / 1 pound white granulated sugar

4 pounds sour cherries

1 Campden tablet

1 teaspoon yeast nutrient

½ teaspoon acid blend

½ teaspoon pectic enzyme

⅛ teaspoon tannin

2 teaspoons (1 packet) dry champagne yeast

3 tablespoons / 1 ounce corn sugar dissolved in ½ cup boiling water and cooled, for bottling

1 • Sanitize a 2-gallon bucket, its lid, the air lock, and a spoon for stirring.

2 • Bring the water to a simmer and stir in the sugar. Stir just until the sugar dissolves and then remove from heat. Let stand until cooled to room temperature.

3 • Pour the sugar water into the 2-gallon bucket. Pit and coarsely chop the cherries, secure the fruit (and pits if using) in a mesh bag, and add to the liquid. Using a potato masher or very clean hands, mash the submerged bag of fruit to extract as much juice as possible. Take a hydrometer reading to determine the original gravity (see Brewer's Handbook, page 16). Crush the Campden tablet and stir it in. Snap on the lid and attach the air lock. Wait 24 hours for the Campden to sterilize the fruit.

4 • After the cherries are sterilized, prepare the yeast starter. Sanitize a measuring cup, a 1-quart canning jar, and a stirring spoon. Scoop out 1 cup of the fruity liquid and pour it into the canning jar. Pour the yeast over top and cover the jar with a piece of plastic wrap secured with a rubber band. Give the jar a good shake and let it stand for 1 to 3 hours. It should become foamy, and you will see tiny bubbles popping on the surface of the liquid. Once you see some sign of activity, the starter can be used.

continued

SPARKLING SOUR CHERRY WINE, CONTINUED

5 • Pour the starter into the fermentation bucket along with the yeast nutrient, acid blend, pectic enzyme, and tannin. Stir vigorously to distribute the yeast and aerate the wine. Snap the lid back on and reattach the air lock. You should see active fermentation as evidenced by bubbles in the air lock within 48 hours.

6 • Let the wine ferment for 1 week, stirring daily with a sanitized spoon. After this time, the wine is ready to transfer into a 1-gallon jug for the secondary fermentation.

7 • Sanitize a 1-gallon jug, its stopper, a strainer, a funnel, a flour sack towel or cheesecloth, and a long-handled spoon. Pull out the bag of cherries with clean hands and squeeze gently to extract as much juice as possible.

8 • Insert the funnel into the 1-gallon jug and line it with the cloth. Slowly pour the wine into the jug, filtering out the solids. Use the spoon as necessary to stir up the sediment that collects in the funnel. Seal the jug with its stopper and insert the air lock.

9 • Let the wine sit somewhere cool and dark for another 4 weeks. You can bottle the wine now or continue aging it for up to 6 months.

10 • If you are continuing to age, it's good to occasionally rack the wine off the sediment that collects on the bottom of the jug. Sanitize a stockpot, the siphon hose, the racking cane, and its tip. Siphon the wine into the stockpot. Clean and sanitize the jug, stopper, and air lock, and siphon the wine back into the jug. Insert the stopper and air lock. You can sample the wine and adjust the acid or tannins to your taste during this step.

11 • To bottle and carbonate, sanitize a stockpot, ten 12-ounce beer bottles or six 22-ounce beer bottles, their caps, the siphon hose, the racking cane, its tip, the bottle filler, and a hydrometer. Siphon ½ cup of wine to the hydrometer and use to determine final gravity. Drink the wine or pour it back into the jug once used.

12 • Pour the corn sugar solution into the stockpot. Siphon the wine into the stockpot to mix with the corn sugar solution, splashing as little as possible. Siphon the wine into bottles, cap, and label.

13 • Let the bottles sit at room temperature out of direct sunlight for at least 2 weeks to fully carbonate. Store for up to 1 year. Serve chilled.

Resources

BREWER'S BOOKSHELF

The Art of Fermentation by Sandor Katz. Info on kefir and kombucha.

Beer Craft: A Simple Guide to Making Great Beer by William Bostwick and Jessi Rymill. A visual guide to beer-brewing and great resource for crafting your own recipes.

Brooklyn Brew Shop's Beer Making Book: 52 Seasonal Recipes for Small Batches by Erica Shea and Stephen Valand. A whole year's worth of fun 1-gallon recipes.

The Complete Guide to American Sake, Sake Breweries, and Homebrewing by Fred Eckhardt. A highly detailed and technical guide to sake homebrewing.

The Complete Meadmaker by Ken Schramm. Mead-making from the bees to the bottle.

Homemade Soda by Andrew Schloss. You will never lack for soda-making inspiration with this book on your shelf.

The Joy of Home Brewing by Charlie Papazian . This is the homebrewer's bible. Its pages contain all the beer-brewing knowledge you could want and more.

The Joy of Home Winemaking by Terry Garey. For in-depth info on wine-making.

BREWER'S SUPPLIERS

Brooklyn Brew Shop

Available at Whole Foods and online: www.brooklynbrewshop.com Complete 1-gallon brewing equipment kits and all-grain mixes.

Cultures for Health

www.culturesforhealth.com Kefir grains and kombucha scobys.

Home Brew Sake

www.homebrewsake.com All sake-brewing supplies, including sake-milled rice and prepared koji.

Kombucha Brooklyn

Available at Williams-Sonoma stores and online: www.kombuchabrooklyn.com Kombucha-brewing kits.

MoreBeer and MoreWine

Available at retail locations throughout the San Francisco Bay Area and online: www.morebeer.com; www.morewinemaking.com General homebrewing supplies. Tell 'em I sent you!

Northern Brewer

Available at Midwestern retail locations and online: www.northernbrewer.com General homebrewing supplies (especially 2-gallon buckets).

Penzeys Spices

Available at retail locations and online: www.penzeys.com High-quality spices.

Measurement Conversions

VOLUME

U.S.	Imperial	Metric
1 tablespoon	$^1/_2$ fl oz	15 ml
2 tablespoons	1 fl oz	30 ml
$^1/_4$ cup	2 fl oz	60 ml
$^1/_3$ cup	3 fl oz	90 ml
$^1/_2$ cup	4 fl oz	120 ml
$^2/_3$ cup	5 fl oz ($^1/_4$ pint)	150 ml
$^3/_4$ cup	6 fl oz	180 ml
1 cup	8 fl oz ($^1/_3$ pint)	240 ml
1 $^1/_4$ cups	10 fl oz ($^1/_2$ pint)	300 ml
2 cups (1 pint)	16 fl oz ($^2/_3$ pint)	480 ml
2 $^1/_2$ cups	20 fl oz (1 pint)	600 ml
1 quart	32 fl oz (1 $^2/_3$ pints)	1 l

TEMPERATURE

Fahrenheit	Celsius/Gas Mark
250°F	120°C/gas mark $^1/_2$
275°F	135°C/gas mark 1
300°F	150°C/gas mark 2
325°F	160°C/gas mark 3
350°F	180 or 175°C/gas mark 4
375°F	190°C/gas mark 5
400°F	200°C/gas mark 6
425°F	220°C/gas mark 7
450°F	230°C/gas mark 8
475°F	245°C/gas mark 9
500°F	260°C

LENGTH

Inch	Metric
$^1/_4$ inch	6 mm
$^1/_2$ inch	1.25 cm
$^3/_4$ inch	2 cm
1 inch	2.5 cm
6 inches ($^1/_2$ foot)	15 cm
12 inches (1 foot)	30 cm

WEIGHT

U.S./Imperial	Metric
$^1/_2$ oz	15 g
1 oz	30 g
2 oz	60 g
$^1/_4$ lb	115 g
$^1/_3$ lb	150 g
$^1/_2$ lb	225 g
$^3/_4$ lb	350 g
1 lb	450 g

Acknowledgments

To my husband, Scott: Thank you for your unwavering support, your supertasting abilities on which I have come to rely, and most of all, your love.

To my parents, Joyce and Dean; my brother, Andy, and his wife, Darci; my family-in-law, Evelyn, Jesse and Bonnie, Russ and Ingrid: You are my family and I love you. Your support this past year has meant the world.

To my agent, Jennifer Griffin: You are awesomeness incarnate. Period.

To my team at Ten Speed Press, Lisa Westmoreland, Jenny Wapner, Betsy Stromberg, Katy Brown, and Kristin Casemore: You gave this book a life of its own beyond what I could have imagined and surpassing all expectations. I am honored to work with you.

To Paige Green, photographer extraordinaire: Thank you for telepathically receiving my vision for the book and then upping the ante of incredible even higher.

To Karen Shinto, food-styling magician: Thank you for taking on the challenge of these crazy, wacky homebrews and making them shine.

To Esther Feinman, prop stylist guru: Thank you for magically finding the perfect glass, bowl, or napkin for every shot.

To Faith Durand, Sara Kate Gillingham-Ryan, and the rest of my cohorts at The Kitchn: You inspire me, lift me up, and make me smile every day. Thank you.

To Robin Davis: I can trace this whole project back to your gentle nudging and enthusiastic support. I can never thank you enough.

To the crew at MoreBeer—Sean, Gary, Joe, and Richard: I have no idea what you first thought of the little blondie who walked into your store, but I'm glad you let me stay. Your opinions and suggestions on my recipes have been invaluable.

To my cadre of recipe testers, Angelina and Philip Williamson, Delia and Richard Lam, Ellen Sherrill, Sarah Rosado, Sabrina Modelle, Gretchen Graham, Eric Mahlstedt, Nicholas Vasilakes, Tom Shaffer, Chris Harrington, J. D. Handley, Omar Gonzalez, Trevor Gowans, James Messick, Ryan McBride, Charlie Collins, Laura Phillips, and Linda Ralleca: You guys rock my world.

In fact, you *all* rock my world. Thank you times infinity.

EMMA CHRISTENSEN is a food writer, beer reviewer, and homebrewer living in the San Francisco Bay Area. She is a recipe editor for the popular home cooking website, The Kitchn (www.thekitchn.com), and a graduate of the Cambridge School of Culinary Arts in Cambridge, Massachusetts. Emma previously worked as the beer reviewer for Ohio's *Columbus Dispatch* and wrote a twice-monthly syndicated recipe column for Tribune Media Services for several years before turning to editing and cookbook writing. To learn more, visit http://emmaelizabethchristensen.blogspot.com.

DANIELLE TSI

A

ACE Cider, 67
Acid blend, 5
Aging, 13
Air locks, 9
Alcohol
    in kefirs, 26
    in kombuchas, 26
    measuring, 16
    in sakes, 145
    in sodas, 26
Amber Ale, 97–99
Apples
    Dry Apple Cider, 73–74
    Sweet Spiced Mulled Cider, 75–76
Apricot Wheat Ale, 104–6

B

Back-sweetening, 71
Banana-Berry Kefir Smoothie, 57
Batch size, increasing, 18
Beers
    adding fruit flavor to, 121
    Amber Ale, 97–99
    Apricot Wheat Ale, 104–6
    brewing terms for, 88
    expert interview for, 87
    Gluten-Free Pale Ale, 111–13
    hops for, 5–6, 93
    improving, 87
    IPA, 101–3
    Jamaican Ginger Beer, 82–83
    malted grains for, 3–4, 96
    Master Beer Recipe, 88–94
    Mocha Stout, 115–17
    Saison Farmhouse Ale, 107–9
    storing, 19
    trickiest part of making, 87

Benary, Oron, 119
Blackberries
    Blackberry-Sage Kombucha, 46
    Blackberry Wine, 164–65
Blueberries
    Banana-Berry Kefir Smoothie, 57
    Blueberry-Lavender Mead, 134–35
    Blueberry-Pomegranate Wine, 169–70
Boil, definition of, 88
Bottle brushes, 12
Bottle cappers, 11–12
Bottle fillers, 12
Bottles
    caps for, 11
    exploding, 18–19
    types of, 11
Bottling
    benefits of, 13
    equipment for, 11–12
    procedure for, 17
    for sodas, 23, 31
Brewing
    equipment for, 8–9
    ingredients for, 3–7
    legality of, 18
    safety of, 18
    steps for, 13
    temperature and, 19
Brothers Drake Meadery, 119
Buckets, 10

C

Cacao nibs
    Mocha Stout, 115–17
Campden tablets, 5
Canning jars, 10
Cantaloupe
    Summer Melon Wine, 171–72

Carbonation, 17
Chai-Spiced Mead, 125–26
Cheesecloth, 8
Cherries
    Cherry-Lime Soda, 30–31
    Cherry, Pistachio, and Cardamom Kefir
        Smoothie, 57
    Cloudy Cherry Sake, 149–50
    Sparkling Sour Cherry Wine, 173–74
Childs, Eric, 37
Chlorine, 14–15
Ciders
    adding fruit flavor to, 121
    Dry Apple Cider, 73–74
    expert interview for, 67
    Hard Lemonade, 79–81
    improving, 67
    Jamaican Ginger Beer, 82–83
    Master Hard Cider Recipe, 68–70
    Pear Cider, 77–78
    Pineapple–Brown Sugar Cider, 84–85
    storing, 19
    Sweet Spiced Mulled Cider, 75–76
    trickiest part of making, 67
Cloudy Cherry Sake, 149–50
Coconut Water Kefir, 62
Corks, 12, 17
Corn sugar, 4
Cranberry Mead, 132–33
Cups, measuring, 8

D

Dry Apple Cider, 73–74
Dry Mead, 123–24

E

Eckhardt, Fred, 143
Equipment
    for bottling, 11–12
    for brewing, 8–9
    for fermentation, 9–11
    sanitizing, 14
Expert interviews
    Benary, Oron, 119
    Childs, Eric, 37
    Foster, Glenn, 155

Friedman, Jesse, 21
Hamren, Nancy Van Brasch, 51
House, Jeffrey, 67
Lorenz, Greg, 137
Paquette, Dann, 87

F

Fermentation
    equipment for, 9–11
    process of, 1
    temperature and, 19
    troubleshooting, 15–16
Fermenters
    primary, 10, 13
    secondary, 11, 13
Flour sack towels, 8
Food storage containers, 12
Foster, Glenn, 155
Friedman, Jesse, 21
Fruit
    canned, 3
    dried, 3
    flavor, adding, 121
    fresh, 3
    frozen, 3
    juice, 3
    Master Hard Cider Recipe, 68–70
    Master Mead Recipe, 120–22
    Master Soda Recipe, 22–23
    Master Wine Recipe, 156–58
    See also individual fruits
Funnels, 10

G

Ginger
    Ginger Ale, 24
    Ginger-Pear Kefir, 60
    Jamaican Ginger Beer, 82–83
Gin-Infused Sake, 153
Gluten-Free Pale Ale, 111–13
Grapefruit Soda, 34
Grape Soda, 32

H

Hamren, Nancy Van Brasch, 51
Hard Lemonade, 79–81

Hibiscus Kombucha, 45
Honey
    buying, 4
    Honey–Green Tea Kombucha, 47
    as sugar substitute, 4–5
    See also Meads
Hops, 5–6, 93
Hot break, definition of, 88
House, Jeffrey, 67
Hydrometers, 12, 16

I

Ingredients
    listing of, 3–7
    measuring and weighing, 14
IPA, 101–3
Irish moss, 6

J

Jamaican Ginger Beer, 82–83
Jasmine Green Tea Sake, 151
Jugs, glass, 11

K

Kefirs
    alcohol in, 26
    Banana-Berry Kefir Smoothie, 57
    Cherry, Pistachio, and Cardamom Kefir
        Smoothie, 57
    Coconut Water Kefir, 62
    expert interview for, 51
    Ginger-Pear Kefir, 60
    grains, 6
    improving, 51
    Mango Lassi Kefir Smoothie, 59
    Master Milk Kefir Recipe, 53–54
    Master Water Kefir Recipe, 55–56
    milk for, 4
    pausing, 59
    Sparkling Raspberry Kefir Wine, 63–64
    storing, 19
    trickiest part of making, 51
    troubleshooting, 54, 56
    Water Kefir Recovery Brew, 65
Koji rice, 6, 138, 146–47
Kombucha Brooklyn, 37

Kombuchas
    alcohol in, 26
    batch size for, 38
    Blackberry-Sage Kombucha, 46
    expert interview for, 37
    flavoring, 49
    Hibiscus Kombucha, 45
    Honey–Green Tea Kombucha, 47
    improving, 37
    Master Kombucha Recipe, 38–40
    pausing, 40
    Peach Iced Tea Kombucha, 41
    storing, 19
    sugars for, 49
    teas for, 49
    trickiest part of making, 37
    troubleshooting, 39
    White Tea–Pomegranate Kombucha, 48
    See also Scoby

L

Legal issues, 18
Lemons
    Gin-Infused Sake, 153
    Hard Lemonade, 79–81
    Meyer Lemon–Thyme Sake, 152
Limes
    Cherry-Lime Soda, 30–31
Lorenz, Greg, 137

M

Malt extract, dried, 5
Malts, 3–4, 96
Mango Lassi Kefir Smoothie, 59
Mash, definition of, 88
Master recipes
    Master Beer Recipe, 88–94
    Master Hard Cider Recipe, 68–70
    Master Kombucha Recipe, 38–40
    Master Mead Recipe, 120–22
    Master Milk Kefir Recipe, 53–54
    Master Sake Recipe #1 (Easy), 138–39
    Master Sake Recipe #2 (Advanced),
        143–45
    Master Soda Recipe, 22–23

Master Water Kefir Recipe, 55–56
Master Wine Recipe, 156–58
Meads
    adding fruit flavor to, 121
    Blueberry-Lavender Mead, 134–35
    Chai-Spiced Mead, 125–26
    corking, 17
    Cranberry Mead, 132–33
    Dry Mead, 123–24
    expert interview for, 119
    improving, 119
    Master Mead Recipe, 120–22
    Renaissance Fair Sweet Mead, 128–29
    storing, 19
    trickiest part of making, 119
    Vanilla Peach Mead, 130–31
Measuring, 8, 14
Melon
    Summer Melon Wine, 171–72
    Watermelon-Mint Soda, 29
Meyer Lemon–Thyme Sake, 152
Milk, 4. *See also* Kefirs
Mocha Stout, 115–17

N

Nancy's Yogurt, 51

O

Orange Cream Soda, 27

P

Paquette, Dann, 87
Peaches
    Peach Iced Tea Kombucha, 41
    Vanilla Peach Mead, 130–31
Pears
    Ginger-Pear Kefir, 60
    Pear Cider, 77–78
Pectic enzyme, 7
Pineapple–Brown Sugar Cider, 84–85
Pitch, definition of, 88
Plum Wine, 159–60
Pomegranates
    Blueberry-Pomegranate Wine, 169–70
    White Tea–Pomegranate Kombucha, 48
Pretty Things Beer and Ale Project, 87

R

Racking canes, 11
Raspberries
    Raspberry-Rhubarb Wine, 166–67
    Sparkling Raspberry Kefir Wine, 63–64
Recipes, scaling, 18
Renaissance Fair Sweet Mead, 128–29
Rhubarb
    Raspberry-Rhubarb Wine, 166–67
Rice
    koji, 6, 138, 146–47
    preparing, for sake, 140
    types of, 4
    See also Sakes
Root Beer, 35

S

Safety, 18
Saison Farmhouse Ale, 107–9
SakéOne, 137
Sakes
    adjusting finished, 150
    alcohol in, 145
    Cloudy Cherry Sake, 149–50
    expert interview for, 137
    Gin-Infused Sake, 153
    improving, 137
    Jasmine Green Tea Sake, 151
    Master Sake Recipe #1 (Easy), 138–39
    Master Sake Recipe #2 (Advanced),
        143–45
    Meyer Lemon–Thyme Sake, 152
    rice for, 4, 6, 138, 140, 146–47
    storing, 19
    trickiest part of making, 137
Sanitizing, 8, 14
Scales, electronic, 8
Scoby
    definition of, 7, 37
    making, 42
    troubleshooting, 39
Siphons, 11, 16–17
Smells, funky, 19
SodaCraft, 21

TRUE BREWS

Sodas
  alcohol in, 26
  bottling, 23, 31
  Cherry-Lime Soda, 30–31
  expert interview for, 21
  Ginger Ale, 24
  Grapefruit Soda, 34
  Grape Soda, 32
  improving, 21
  Master Soda Recipe, 22–23
  Orange Cream Soda, 27
  overcarbonated, 30
  Root Beer, 35
  storing, 19
  Strawberry Soda, 26
  sugar-free, 24
  trickiest part of making, 21
  Watermelon-Mint Soda, 29
Sparge, definition of, 88
Sparkling Raspberry Kefir Wine, 63–64
Sparkling Sour Cherry Wine, 173–74
Spoons
  long-handled, 8
  measuring, 8
Stockpots, 9
Strainers, fine-mesh, 8, 9
Strawberries
  Banana-Berry Kefir Smoothie, 57
  Strawberry Soda, 26
  Strawberry Wine, 162–63
Sugars
  bottling, 88
  nonfermentable, 71
  types of, 4–5
Summer Melon Wine, 171–72
Sweet Spiced Mulled Cider, 75–76

T
Talon Wine Brands, 155
Tannin, 7
Tea
  Chai-Spiced Mead, 125–26
  Jasmine Green Tea Sake, 151
  See also Kombuchas
Tepache, 84
Thermometers, 9

V
Vanilla Peach Mead, 130–31

W
Water
  dechlorinating, 14–15
  filtering, 5
Water Kefir Recovery Brew, 65
Watermelon-Mint Soda, 29
White Tea–Pomegranate Kombucha, 48
Wine corkers, 11–12
Wines
  adding fruit flavor to, 121
  Blackberry Wine, 164–65
  Blueberry-Pomegranate Wine, 169–70
  corking, 17
  expert interview for, 155
  improving, 155
  Master Wine Recipe, 156–58
  Plum Wine, 159–60
  Raspberry-Rhubarb Wine, 166–67
  Sparkling Raspberry Kefir Wine, 63–64
  Sparkling Sour Cherry Wine, 173–74
  storing, 19
  Strawberry Wine, 162–63
  Summer Melon Wine, 171–72
  trickiest part of making, 155
Wort, definition of, 88

Y
Yeast
  nutrient, 7
  for sodas, 22
  starter, 14–15
  temperature and, 19
  types of, 5